The "UNKNOWN" Culture Club ✈

Korean Adoptees, Then and Now

**Arranged & Designed
by the Vance Twins**

Copyright
© 2015 Against Child Trafficking USA
All rights reserved.
ISBN-13: 978-1512331530
ISBN-10: 1512331538

DEDICATION

To all families of adoption-loss, adopted people, and supporters.
You are not alone. You have a right to speak.
You have a right to be heard.

We extend appreciation to the contributors
for granting reprint permission.
We give special thanks to Allen L. Vance;
Book Cover Graphic Designer, Dustin Vance;
and Acquisitions Editor, Katherine Kim.

For Joseph Tae Holt (1952-1984)

This collection was pulled together from a 2014 call of submissions for people adopted from Korea. All contributions were welcomed. This newest edition, *The "Unknown" Culture Club: Korean Adoptees, Then and Now,* is a continuation of the Vance Twins' social justice work and book three in a compilation called, *The rEvolutionary Orphan Series.* The Vance Twins would like to point out that the stories within this anthology are *not* intended to be used as examples of adoption trafficking but are experiences courageously shared in the effort to inform isolated adoptees (who might be deprived of an empathetic upbringing), that there is a diverse, yet unified network of people who can identify and truly understand the ups-and-downs of adoption—*because we have lived it.* Contributors have shared memories to the best of their ability. The narratives do not necessarily represent their thoughts about adoption at moment, the editors or the publisher. Since the Korean War ended, adoption facilitators have processed at least 200,000 Korean children and continue to do so today. The practice has spread worldwide. Narratives from global adopted people and families of adoption-loss can be found in the subsequent book, *Adoptionland: From Orphans to Activists.*

✈

PART ONE
PAST "UNKNOWN"

IT'S OUR TURN NOW

1. **LIFE SWAP**
Janine Myung Ja ✈1

2. **JOURNEY OF A THOUSAND MILES**
Lee, Dug-Won ✈5

3. **THE PASTOR'S KID**
Darius X ✈11

4. **OUTSIDE, LOOKING IN**
David Han ✈17

5. **DEPORTED**
Monte Haines ✈29

6. **BEHIND THE SMILE**
Kelli Buhr ✈35

PART TWO
CULTURE "UNKNOWN"

7. THE BLIND GIRL
Blair King ✈47

8. FINDING A FAMILY
Shannon Doona Heit ✈51

9. GOING BACK
Khara Nine ✈59

10. LETTER FROM GRANDMOTHER
Robin Högberg ✈65

11. REMEMBER ME
Danielle Godon-Decoteau ✈73

12. SOME SCARS ARE WORN ON THE INSIDE
Simone Rendon Lutz ✈81

13. THIS IS MY BIRTH FATHER
Christina Seong ✈88

✈

PART THREE
CLUB "UNKNOWN"

14. BECOMING REAL
Patty Sang ✈93

15. BURIED ROOTS
Jessica Sun Lee ✈99

16. KILLING ME SOFTLY WITH NO WORDS
Joo, Hyun ✈105

17. DUALITY
Kathryn Lustig ✈109

18. REFLECTIONS OF SEOUL
Hanna Sofia Jung Johansson ✈111

19. MESSAGE ON COLORBLIND PARENTING
Mark Hagland ✈115

PART FOUR
FUTURE "UNKNOWN"

20. I CAN'T GO ON NOT KNOWING
Kim Yang Ai aka "E" ✈121

21. I TRULY BELIEVED THEY WERE MY REAL FAMILY
Adam Crapser ✈129

21. I DID NOT EXIST IN THEIR DATA BANK
Sonja Suh ✈135

23. BORN AT THE AIRPORT
Kim Goudreau ✈143

24. THE WAKE-UP CALL
Jin Vilsgaard ✈149

25. I CAN'T DO NOTHING AND CALL IT PEACE
Janine Myung Ja ✈157

ORPHAN'S MOUNT

PART ONE:

PAST "UNKNOWN"

IT'S OUR TURN NOW

I've been stuck-
-stuck for so long.
I've been listening to you,
[Dad and Mom]
trying to get strong.
Self doubt told me
I've been wrong to sing my own song,
so I've been using yours—not mine,
I've been following along.
Not being a leader,
I've been singing *your* song.

Today, though, a voice
Reveals another way:
It's your choice, my dear.
It's your choice to use your voice,
your magical,
mystical,
mysterious
voice.

The call of the wild resides in you,
you can do what you choose,
but use your voice when you do,
a voice inside—
inside of you.
Can you hear
your heart
the art,
the beat of a different drum,
a drum that belongs to you?

It's *my turn now*,
To change things 'round.
It's *my turn now*,
To make a choice.
It's *my turn now*,
to use my voice.

It's our turn now

✈ *Janine Myung Ja*

INTRODUCTON

When most of us think about adoption, we see adoring images of lonely children commonly referred to as "orphans" in the glossy pages of adoption magazines and websites, proud words of wisdom given by devoted adoptive parents, and stories of gratitude. For the past sixty years, the public can't help but assume there is only one adoption narrative and all others are "bad" or "negative." This simply is not true. After being directly engaged in the worldwide adoptee community and after listening to thousands of stories for more than a decade, we know the narratives are as diverse as there are people. Adopted children are now elders. They should now be considered old enough to receive truthful and transparent answers. They should now be old enough to tell their own stories.

Where in the world have the adoption agencies sent 200,000 Korean children and how have these children faired for the last sixty years? After placing us in foreign homes, how many adoption facilitators checked on our status, ensuring our well-being? Has intercounty adoption become a win-win for all? Why can these agencies have access to our origins, but we're forbidden to access that same information? When are we considered "old enough" to know the truth? Why should strangers (even if they are employees) have more information on our ancestry than any of us? And for those of us with birth siblings, why did employees fail to include (and/or refuse to disclose) this data within our adoption files? At least then we could have been been connected to a blood relative—and not be so segregated.

Intercountry adoption pioneers have led the dialogue, developed policy, and built the child welfare system while the public has followed along, fully trusting these folks with the lives of children. Yet, the adopted children—many reaching retirement age now—are still treated as if they need to be protected from their families of origin, their ancestry—given the run-around when they request their adoption file. This veiling and hiding puts them at risk for health issues, too. Come on! How much older do they need to be to know the truth about their origins?

Like all other adopted people, Korean adoptees have many concerns that have yet to be acknowledged by the mainstream in the East and West. Within the pages of this collection—compiled for and by Korean adoptees—these adults, adopted from 1955 and onward, share stories about our unknown status, the culture of adoption within adoptive homes, the shock of deportation, traveling back to Korea for the first time, finding Korean families (who actually do exist), and coming to terms with our ever-changing identities.

If you were in some way abused or not seen for who you truly are, judged by your appearance, treated unfairly, or been the underdog, then this anthology will validate your experiences. You are definitely not the only one who has felt alone and isolated. Thousands of adoptees—not just Korean-born adoptees—have had many challenges to overcome, on top of the treatment they received from bio families, adoptive parents, extended family, strangers, and community. Adoption can create multiple additional burdens.

If you were supposed to be "seen and not heard" and told "you would have died if you hadn't been adopted," you will probably be able to identify with the contributors in this collection. The public is just now realizing that not all birth families are "bad" and not all adoptive families are "good." It seems obvious

THE "UNKNOWN" CULTURE CLUB

now, but sixty years ago, when intercountry adoption was being pioneered in the East, most adoption facilitators made racist assumptions about foreign nations and their family dynamics, and few questioned these misinterpretations and misunderstandings. We, the adopted ones, have had to live the consequences.

In order for the community to claim the peace we deserve, we need to investigate further. My sister and I have joined the child rights dialogue and we are now informed on the United Nations Convention on the Rights of the Child (UNCRC). (Funny how Child Rights Activists do not intentionally want to know about the current state of affairs. We simply fell into it and then we felt compelled to help our fellow sisters and brothers out, someway, somehow.)

On top of varying family dynamics, included within this collection are just a few of the concerns adult adopted people must address. These experiences were destined to be heard—if not compiled by us, then by someone else. We have found this community to be perceptive, insightful, empathetic, wanting to correct injustices, and now awareness to the problem is spreading all over the world. We remain rooted in nature—because that's truly who we are and how our interests are related.

Welcome to the club.

✈ **THE VANCE TWINS**

1

LIFE SWAP

When I was a preteen, my American adoptive father sustained a traumatic brain injury caused by a 100-foot fall from hang gliding, an accident that left him "permanently disabled" (—or at least that's how other people have categorized him. In my opinion, he just does things differently now—but that's another story.) I remember watching my American adoptive mom try to cope with the loss. He had been a reputable and educated husband, an engineer and a Presbyterian church elder. Suddenly, Dad lost his impressive career and, instead, had to concentrate for years on learning to walk, talk, dress, groom, and feed himself. I so wanted to find a way to end my parents' grief. This quandary gave me purpose as young as age twelve. I almost became obsessed with the idea of finding solutions for my parents' pain. (Maybe this is an adoptee attribute? Yet, I did not give my adoption-status a glimmer of thought back then in 1984.)

Before Dad's injury, both parents were hoarders. No one knew this about Mom and Dad—not even the neighbors. In the late 1950s, Dad began to build the 4,000-square-foot house with a black fence to surround their property which would provide privacy and protection. Behind the gates, by the time we kids came along, the property resembled a junkyard assortment of moss-covered vintage Cadillac limousines, sports cars, a GMC motorhome, a motorcycle, and other fixer-uppers—fourteen vehicles in total (even two Jaguars were stored in the basement workshop). These vehicles were parked in the front yard and down the hill to the back. Today, at age eighty-five, Dad likes to joke that we kids (my sister and two brothers) thought the rec room was a place to store wrecked cars.

Mom packed the family home with her own stuff, such as name-brand goods that were on sale and belongings she could not say "no" to and did not have the heart to toss once their shelf lives expired. All of this stuff spilled out of cardboard boxes (hence the title of my first book *Twins Found in a Box: Adapting to Adoption*) and plastic tubs, which were stacked and lined up along the hallways and in living spaces. We kids didn't mind the mess. We thought it was normal and paid no mind to it.

On the surface and behind the fence, we appeared to be the perfect all-American family—the type adoption magazines proudly labeled and promoted as a *Forever Family*. But, my sister and I knew that not everything is as it appears on the surface. It didn't take long for us to figure that out.

More grief filled the household five years after Dad's accident and just before my twin and I were about to graduate from high school in 1989. Mom was diagnosed with cancer. There was a point during high school when she couldn't stand having my sister and me around the house and that's when we moved in with our boyfriends. Between school and minimum wage jobs, we would ride our bikes to our adoptive parents' home to spy on Dad in a desperate attempt to check on his well-being. Mom was too tired to take care of him, and their marriage dwindled down to an impending divorce. Dad felt isolated, neglected, and unheard. Reduced to the label "incompetent," he believed his life to be useless. Dad adamantly opposed Mom's divorce petition, claiming such an act was "against God."

Disagreements ensued for the next seven years, resulting in Mom's word against Dad's, false claims of incompetency against him, and finally an unfair separation which lasted until my mid-twenties. Heavily influenced by my religious upbringing back then, I wondered, "When parents disagree, which parent are the children supposed to honor?" Especially when both parents profess to be the better and more loyal Christian? By the time 1997 rolled around, my father had read the Bible cover-to-cover thirty-two times. Yet, Mom had been the church organist for many years, came from a Christian family, and we kids knew we should never argue with her.

Despite "keeping up with the Joneses" (and exceeding) and looking like respectable church leaders, our adoptive parents weren't as perfect as we kids assumed they were prior to Dad's injury. We didn't hold this against them, of course. They held their own secrets and for thirty years into their marriage, both remained quiet on a couple issues. It wasn't until the last months of Mom's life in 1997 that Dad had the audacity to tell the truth and flip our world upside-down.

From our parents' arguments and during their drawn-out divorce, we learned there are always two sides to every story. This could be the reason we saw under the surface of things so easily when it came to intercountry adoption. My twin and I felt compelled to learn more about the authentic lives of real people and we always loved to hear what other people were saying. This strong curiosity motivated us to initiate a social media group called, "Adoption Truth and Transparency Worldwide Network," which now—surprisingly—has almost 6,000 members.

My twin and I weren't the only ones with questions about adoption ethics! This group led to the compilation of *Adoptionland: From Orphans to Activists*, written for and by adopted people and parents-of-loss from around the world. Becoming engaged in the adoption community has led me to discover that families of orphans do exist (they've just been left behind). In fact, for every forever family built by adoption, another family is forever torn.

After listening to the "confidential" side of adoption (adoptee voices originating from Africa to Asia, the US and Europe), I still believe these individuals need to be heard. And when I learned that adoptees—especially those sent to abusive situations—are shamed and scolded to "be quiet" about their varied experiences, I've become even more concerned. Most shocking for me has been watching adult adoptees be persecuted by individuals who react in a knee-jerk way, and then immediately labeled and branded in one fell swoop as: "anti-adoption," "anti-Christian," and even "anti-God." I was floored. This treatment brought to mind the way my adoptive father was reduced to a label, being marginalized, ignored, and abandoned during the divorce.

Just because I questioned exactly how I was relinquished for adoption, I have been bullied, pigeon-holed, and accused of being unable to hold an intelligent conversation by those who put their full trust in adoption facilitators. Even before my research into the practice, the first adoptive mother to antagonize me, pointed an accusatory finger at my chest and scolded me at a bookfest, "You should be ashamed of yourself," referring to my book, *The Search for Mother Missing*. This mother hadn't even read it yet, but nonetheless reacted hastily, making claims that I was "anti-this" or "anti-that" after finding out that I had been adopted. She also made the kneejerk assumption that I wasn't thankful enough. At that time, I didn't know I had a right to ask tough questions and hold persecutors accountable. Still in my thirties, a naive and newly published author who knew very little about how harsh the pro-adoptive parent community could be, I hid my book under a bushel (or in the back of the closet) for the next decade after I got home from what was supposed to be a celebratory event.

Another discreet incident made me shrink even further into self-doubt. I had been invited to attend a Fourth of July parade by a writer friend in what's called "God's country" here in the US (rural areas barely touched by foreigners—people like me). While loitering around the author's table, I noticed an adoptive mother and her adopted daughter run-walk by me, and as they passed the mother used one of her hands to cover the eyes of her little Asian daughter. How insulting. It was as if the mother felt the need to "protect" her daughter from the likes of me—a "real" Asian-American female. I knew because at one time I had been that little protected girl—shielded from the bad influences of anything foreign. *I've walked that walk.* You will read here, others have too.

✈ **JANINE MYUNG JA**

2

JOURNEY OF A THOUSAND MILES

My story starts in February of 2003. I had sold my house in Seattle, Washington and while removing my stuff, I pilfered through an old cardboard box of junk in the basement. In it, I spotted a beat-up and dog-chewed book belonging to my adoptive parents: *The Seed From the East* by Bertha Holt. Bertha recalled her late husband's time in Korea and the adoption of eight Amerasian children motivated by watching a World Vision movie. The memoir detailed how the Holt's strong belief in God inspired them to look for more GI war babies—children with American fathers and Korean mothers—and bring them home to the United States. Their work became a gateway to Adoption by Proxy and led to the setting up of Korea's Child Welfare Program.

I skimmed through it. After two days, I set down the memoir consumed by its contents. This book was describing me. The light bulb switched on: children who had my kind of life in Korea. The thought hit me so hard, it ignited my journey into learning more about my Korean heritage—something I had ignored for five decades.

I spent hours at the computer reading everything I could about anything related to adopted Amerasian kids like me, and then I thought about my Korean mother and the Korean War, drawing upon as much information as possible from the internet. I studied the subject late into the night and for many nights after. I immediately wrote the Holts to ask about my adoption files but, disappointingly, they gave me very limited answers. I continued to read anything I could get my hands on.

I decided to go to the Holt's summer picnic in Eugene, Oregon. There, I met Susan Cox, also adopted from South Korea. We were happy to meet each other. Prior to that meeting, it felt as if I was the only Amerasian adoptee. She immediately told me to stick around and afterwards we exchanged information and stories. I told her I was # 306 RC William McNair and she understood what that meant. Susan recommended that I attend a meeting with the Adult Asian Adoptees of Washington. There I met Tim Holm, another Amerasian adoptee who lived in the same city. It took me until October to do that, but when I finally did, my world was rocked, and I was immediately accepted into the Korean adoptee community. Tim told me about an upcoming adoptee gathering held in Seoul. *Well, I was there.*

I always had a faint memory of being left at the orphanage as a screaming four-and-a-half year old boy. I remember a woman's hand clutching mine inside a reception center, and then she suddenly released her grasp. In my mind, I remember her crying and rushing away. I hollered after her: "Omma. Omma. Omma." The memory of her leaving me there and taking off has haunted me for many days throughout my life.

At fifty-years-old, I started searching deeper into my origin, while preparing to go to Korea. I had contacted Global Overseas Adoptees Link (GOAL) who put my story in the paper and then I met with the Korean Broadcasting Station Program Director for help to look into my adoption file, which I had forwarded to her from World Vision. Once I arrived in Seoul, South Korea, I met the director for coffee inside a Starbucks and with the help of a translator, an English teacher who lived in Seoul, I was told that they found amazing information for me. They found my original birth village of Pa Joon Kun now called Paju City. They had found six people who had known my Korean mother and me!

They also told me my birth name, which contrasted with the name in my adoption file. I wasn't Cho-Johnny and my mother wasn't Cho, Soon-Bak as documented. The Program Director said Cho, Soon-Bak was like my second omma (mother) ... an older friend of my mother's who delivered me to the reception center after my mother's death. My omma's name was Lee, Jung-Sook and she had named me Lee, Dug-Won. She was fifteen years old when she had me. My American father, a GI, was known as Johnny. My omma wanted me to stay in Korea forever, and loved me very much.

I have a strong recollection of being carried on her back as a small child in the traditional way mothers carry their children. I remember riding on my omma's back even until age three and four, and I remember her scent because I was so close to her. Along Korea's greenery and hills, she didn't want to put me down because of the fear of predators or the possibility of people grabbing me. She kept me close with her until she died at age eighteen or nineteen from a lung problem.

At about age three or four, I was passed around from one army nurse to another until I was given to my mother's friend Cho, Soon-Bak. She was the one who had changed my name to Cho-Johnny, and escorted me to World Vision. The Army Chaplain, William McNair, immediately delivered me to Holt's Reception Center on the same day, October 2nd, 1957.

The week before the 2004 Adoptee Gathering in Seoul, I was taken to Paju, my birthtown to visit with a few elder folks who remembered me. At first they didn't want to say too much but then one came forth subsequent to studying the photos of me as a small child and as an adult. This stirred forth more information. One of the residents, a *halmoni*, an elder woman, was very emotional when she spoke to me, although it was in Korean and I could not understand. Fortunately, the translator could interpret for us. The *halmoni* touched my hair, my face and my neck to show how fond she was of my arrival and then divulged the difficulties of post-war life. Crying tears of endearment and perhaps for many lost years, she wanted to hug and hold me, and when it was time to go, she begged me to stay.

Korean Adoptees, Then and Now

The other elder villagers told me a story about a little white boy and a little black boy who were born and lived in the village at one time and I was the little white boy. They recalled that we actually lived in the hills, close to the army base. My mother would take me with her to visit the base a few days throughout the week and we often stayed there overnight.

At last, during this visit to my village of origin, the Korean folks led me to my mother's grave where I was able to honor and bow to her. I was shocked to learn so much about my young life in Korea. Everything I found was like a miracle to me.

Recollections

I arrived in the United States, a scared little four-year-old boy on Thanksgiving, November 28th 1957. I remembered sitting on the left side of the airplane as it arrived in Seattle to deliver eight of us children to our new families. The adults came for me and I knew that life was about to take a drastic change. While departing the airplane, I held onto the hand of the little girl who had sat next to me on the plane. There was a feeling of no control over this migration onto new soil. Both scared, the little girl and I disembarked and descended the stairs toward the airport tarmac. So many unfamiliar faces staring at us and they were speaking a different language—English! So confusing! We had no idea what would happen. At first afraid of these unknown people, I couldn't help but to cry at the foreign sight.

I was handed to an American couple who became my adoptive parents and with the help of their son, who was eight years older than me, I was taken to a stand and given a toy truck. This helped to ease the stress for the moment and gave me something to focus my attention on.

We left the airport and arrived at a house above a laundromat, which belonged to my adoptive father's side of the family. I remember my first Thanksgiving. I but reached tabletop level, and my curious eyes stared at the platters brimming with the turkey and large dishes of stuffing, sweet potatoes and mashed potatoes while I lingered around the dining room. I kept staring at all the food. I didn't know a word of English so I couldn't communicate with the grown-ups or the children.

Remembering back, I was placed in a very lonely, dysfunctional, trauma-filled household. My adoptive parents were alcoholics, and my dad was a compulsive gambler. I remember being told by my father's side of the family that they were going to send me back to where I had come from. Even my paternal adoptive grandmother told me this. I heard terrible things about my Korean mother who they referred to as a "f—cking whore."

My adoptive family for me was a big mistake. I was always reminded that Korea was terrible place and the country threw me away. Later, my cousins revealed that for about a year my adoptive parents had told family members that I was just a neighbor boy. My adoptive brother abused me for about six years and his friends would threaten me. During those initial years, I would hope to get something in the mail with news that my birth mother was coming from Korea to retrieve me.

The racist name-calling by classmates began in first grade. I remember running down the hill after school toward the laundromat and telling my adoptive mother that the school kids were calling me bad names but she brushed it off, telling me: "oh, that's all right, they don't mean it," so I never told anyone again. The taunting lasted until I finished high school and I kept the pain inside, not knowing what the ache within me was ... I just couldn't put my finger on it. There was no one else in the world like me. It was a terrible childhood.

When I became a teenager, I tried to rid the pain with drugs. A bad choice. I ended up in drug rehab, which worked the first time, a blessing. In my late twenties, I straightened up my life and worked very hard to become a firefighter. I did experience racism then, but I always felt good being part of a group. With renewed focus, I finally found something that made me feel good about myself: rescuing and helping people. This became my driving force and gave me a reason to be happy and continue to work hard.

At times I reflect upon my orphan/adoptee life and I know it's not normal, but it's all I have. I have shared part of my story to very few non-adoptees. It's fascinating to them, but for me, it's simply part of who I am. A big part of my life wasn't exactly wonderful, but I know I have been blessed, and have had it better compared to many others. As adoptees go, I have been very fortunate to find a little bit about my Korean mother and our life together. It's allowed me to piece things together, and start the closure I needed in order to enter the healing process. I doubt the pain will be completely healed, but the difference is now I have acceptance for who I am from others like me, and given me clarity about who I am: half Korean and half white. Meeting other Amerasian adoptees has been a fulfilling experience. I now know that I truly belong to a community.

Now I am a retired sixty-one year-old retired firefighter with a twenty-nine year career. My adoptive family—however they were—I do miss. They have all been deceased since 1995. I'm a divorced father, with two grown children, and six grandchildren. They are the family I was always searching for. I am very active in their lives and can fortunately spend time with them a couple of days each week. My constant companion is a mini Schnauzer dog, who was also abandoned. I have close Korean adoptee and native Koreans friends who are like family to me. I'm part of an adoptee group and also spend time on Facebook, staying connected to the adoptee community and especially the HAPA (Amerasian Adoptee) group.

✈ RANDY WEST
LEE DUG-WON

3

THE PASTOR'S KID

Before I became the person that I am today, I had many identities. In no particular order, I've been called: Korean. Orphan. Adoptee. American. Asian American. Slant-Eyes. Flat-Nose. Christian. Shy Kid. Good at drawing. Nail biter. Oriental girl with really long hair. Tom Boy. Honor Student. Piano Student. Potty Mouth. Model Minority. Dyke. Faggot. Drag King. Punk. But before I was any of these things, I was a number. K77-1383 was my case number. And then I became the Pastor's Kid.

My adoptive father was an ordained Lutheran minister. My adoptive mother, who prided herself as a good Christian woman, still believes in the all-American Christian life. Back then it was seen as a radical move for White parents to adopt "kids of color."

It was the 70s. The Civil Rights movement was evolving and protests against the Vietnam War marched on. The young pastor and his wife were a part of a new generation of optimistic and sympathetic Christians who wanted to adopt children from second and third world countries. My charismatic and ambitious adoptive father started his own church by knocking on doors and inviting people to join him for services at a local high school gymnasium. His grass roots leadership paid off and the congregation quickly outgrew the make-shift facilities. Soon he collected enough funds and talent to build a beautiful new church.

My adoptive parents, aka my parents, fostered two Native American sisters but later were not available for adoption.

In 1975, my parents adopted my older brother from Vietnam when he was five years old and unable to speak English. His rotten baby teeth gave evidence of a ravaged war-torn country that fed their orphans sugarcane and rice. In 1977, at five-and-a-half months old, I was adopted from Seoul, South Korea, now the only infant in the family.

By 1982, my parents decided it was time to adopt more kids. I remember I attended only a half day in kindergarten class because we drove to Spokane, Washington to pick up my new sister and little brother.

Why my parents kept my new siblings ethnicity a secret, is a mystery. They had already fostered two Native Americans and adopted two kids from East Asia, and now they proudly added two French/Italian kids to our "rainbow" family. At least the kids were white, like them—well, maybe not Norwegian /Scottish /Irish /German white—but dark skinned white. Mediterranean white. Right?

My black-haired and olive-skin-toned siblings by way of their biological mother, but separated into different foster homes, ethnic ambiguity remained a curiosity and a source of confusing racism from playground bullies. The two grew up believing they might be a mix of French and Italian, but the secret my parents kept was that they were sourced from a large Roma community in Eastern Washington. *Gypsies* is the oppressive word most people used, a racist insult like *Jap* or *Chink*. But we didn't know that. All we knew about "other" cultures and races was from glossy candy-colored Disney movies or whatever we watched on 1980s American TV shows.

My sister found out her true lineage when she was teenager. She dug deep into her and her brother's adoption paperwork and found information that had been blacked out with a marker. Held up to the light, she could see the truth. Typical clinical statistics. Birth date. Weight. Race. Race? Gypsy. Not Caucasian, but Gypsy. My sister was proud to be a Gypsy and still is. At least she knew what to call herself. She finally got to have a small answer to the big questions we all ask: "Who am I?" When my sister questioned our mom about it, she answered, "We were afraid the Gypsies would come and steal you away."

A friend once told me, "Your family is so ordinary and normal." I suppose there's some truth to that but I don't really know what that means. We were protected from outsiders and "safe" in the bubble of church life and parochial schooling and trained from an early age to appear and act normal. But that bubble had to burst at some point.

I had only vaguely heard of manic depression or bi-polar disorder when my father was diagnosed. Nobody expected this to happen. It wasn't until I started to understand the disease that I began to recognize the level of abuse we had experienced. Despite the appearances in church and school, there was a lot of chaos at home. Chaos and mental illness don't mix well.

Here's a social experiment: let's see what happens when you collect a bunch of traumatized orphan kids from around the world and throw them into one crazy family. Who's gonna make it out alive? Blend in or get pushed out. Primal stuff. Survival of the fittest. Lord of the Flies. We had wild imaginations in a tightly controlled world. My little sister and brother fought all the time. Blood is thicker than water, as the saying goes.

One time my little brother pissed me off one too many times and BAM! I just kicked him in the eye. I couldn't help it. And I knew I was gonna' get into big trouble for it. I didn't get in trouble for kicking him, I got in trouble because I kicked him and gave him a black eye and as Mom reminded me, "Tomorrow is Sunday and now I'm going to have to explain to the people at church and that might not look so good for Dad's reputation." It was just kid stuff. The next day at church I kept quiet and smiled. I was rather pleased with my accomplishment, but I had to keep cool. Look normal. Pastor's kids don't act up. We knew we were being watched.

It was always noisy at home. If it wasn't the sounds of fighting then it was the sounds of somebody getting in trouble. And if it wasn't noisy, the silence was a tight-lipped reminder of the tension in the air. Mom suffered from debilitating migraines. I'm sure the noise didn't help. She would hide in her bedroom in complete darkness and cry for days. Dad had several medical emergencies, first came the kidney stones. He also struggled with heart problems and was well aware that his own father had died young from a heart attack. Later came the sudden manic swings and deep suicidal depression. It wouldn't be until I left home for college that he would be treated with a two-year series of electroshock therapy. Ten years later he was diagnosed with brain cancer. It's amazing how we survived. Not very well, auto pilot just kicked in.

The dinner table was the battlefield. As tradition, we always had to have dinner together, of course. After the ritual prayer we participated in routine family conversations about how our day went. Dad sat at the head of the table with his hands folded into a white-knuckled fist. Mom would try to relax his hand as if that would release the rage he held inside.

My sister had a hard time figuring out the rules of the house. Shit, we all did. It was all so bizarre, none of it made sense to us. We had the same table seating each night, which was unfortunate for my sister since she sat next to Dad. Often she sat with her elbows on the table or ate her fingers. One night Dad picked up his fork and stabbed her hand, righteously angered by her poor table manners. As usual, Mom said, "Honey, calm down." She wouldn't defend any of us. He hollered, "Oh, I didn't do it very hard!" and continued the dinner conversation as if nothing had happened. Another time he couldn't handle the bickering anymore. He grabbed my sister and brother's hair and smashed their skulls together, again "not very hard." If there were happy times in my family, I've blanked out most of them. I can't remember if they were forced or genuine.

I came out to my parents on my 25th birthday. There was a sense of urgency with my announcement. I was already nervous before we were seated inside the tiny brunch cafe. It was Mother's Day and the place was packed. My plan of attack was to just spit out the words. Alright already, okay? And Go! I had already come out as Queer way back in high school, but they kind of ignored my "outing" and wanted to believe it was just a phase. I appreciate good timing and I figured age 25 was a good year to start my new life as a man. I was changing my name and pronoun and I needed them to participate. My parents had never really heard of the terms Transgender, Transexuals, and Transvestites. Yeah, they knew about that, but what I was describing was very different from the negative stereotypes my parents envisioned. I was part of a growing movement of Queers and activists who were bucking against our society's oppressive two-gender binary system. I'm sure their eyes glazed over as I preached the virtues of gender non-conforming pronoun etiquette. I don't remember where in the conversation my dad inserted a biblical reference to prostitution. Somehow, somewhere in his mind, there was a connection and I needed to be reminded. Of what, I'm not sure. My dad wasn't a brimstone and hellfire kind of pastor, but when it came to matters relating to female sexuality and power, my sister and I were often victims to his unfounded and random blaming.

They hadn't really gotten used to having a *gay* daughter but now I switched things backwards and upside down. My mom boldly explained that when they adopted me they specifically chose a girl. I didn't fall for the guilt trap. I wasn't going to take responsibility for destroying their idea of a perfectly planned family. I wasn't going to put up with being treated as a "catalog baby" or some kind of trained pet they got from the animal shelter.

The rest of my family, including my grandparents, adjusted to my new gender identity quickly. Grandma was especially intrigued by what kinds of surgeries that Transmen get. When I told her about my desire to get reconstructive chest surgery, she proudly lifted up her shirt to show me her mastectomy scars. Grandpa, concerned about my romantic life, worried that I wouldn't experience sex in the way that men like him enjoyed. I winked and said, "Don't worry Grandpa, I got it covered." Grandma chimed in, "Well, shit. I don't care if you have sex with a stick as long as you're happy!" I love my grandma and I miss her dearly. My other grandpa wrote a touching letter with a simple message: "Congratulations! Way to go MAN!"

The support and love I received from my grandparents was exactly what I needed since my parents were less than understanding. I stopped talking to them and held my silent grudge for years. I didn't need them. I belonged to a global community of

Korean Adoptees, Then and Now

social outcasts: artists, activists, people of color, Queers, Asian-Americans, Adoptees, weirdoes of all stripes. I've adopted them as my own chosen family.

My mom has come a long way since then. She is eternally remorseful for her ignorant and hateful actions towards me. She still slips up occasionally and refers to me as "she" and "her," often in public places. I don't really care anymore, I'm fully bearded and balding and strangers have no clue about the faux pas. She likes to cut out articles about Transgenders and will mail them to me. One year for my birthday she cut out a photo of Cher and Chaz Bono and made a card that said, "Here's an extra ID photo to get into the motel in case we forget ours. Love, Mom." It's adorable and I still keep it by my desk.

Dad passed away in 2013. He had been living in an assisted-living home. The years of mental and physical health problems had made it impossible for my mom to be his primary care giver. She gave it her all even when she suffered from her own mental collapse. She had skeletons in her closet too and eventually had to come out about her addiction to prescription medications. Dad's deteriorated body had been reduced to skin and bones. His speech had become barely audible and indecipherable. I thought it was perfectly ironic since his entire career was built around public speaking and our home life was so verbally toxic. During my last conversations with him, he struggled to form the words, "Are we cool?"

"Yeah I guess," I lied. That's all he would ever get from me. A half lie for a half life.

His memorial service was held at the church he founded. There was pomp and circumstance and rituals I forgot but muscle-memoried into action. I had almost forgotten what it was like to be the Pastor's Kid. Church people who had remembered me as a cute little girl awkwardly reminisced about what a great man my dad was. My dad's cousin was really confused by me and muttered, "Well now I don't remember you. You must have come later?"

I kept quiet and smiled.

✈ **DARIUS X**

4

OUTSIDE, LOOKING IN

My story – Searching for Acceptance and Love

I was born in Tamyang-Gun, Cholla-Hamdo, Republic of Korea. My birth date of March 10th, 1966, is an estimation since the orphanage would not provide information about my Korean parents. The earliest documented record of me is when I was picked up off the street of Kwangju, a city in South Korea, on February 6, 1971.

I lived in an orphanage and in foster homes until I was adopted in October of 1972 by an American couple. My adoptive dad worked as a high school history teacher and attended seminary at night. He would later be ordained as a minister in the Episcopalian Church. My adoptive mother was a high school guidance counselor. They had two biological children: a daughter, six years older than me; and a son, four years older than me. I can't imagine what they must have thought when their parents talked about adopting me, much less what they thought when their parents brought me home, a scrawny malnourished young boy with worms.

My childhood was filled with anger and hate. I was abandoned on a street of a Korean city and left to fend for myself as an orphan. My self-esteem and self-worth got stuck at this point in my life. I have very few friends with whom I allowed myself to open up and show who I truly am. In my mind, I am forever the orphan—accused of stealing, scrounging and begging for food. I still see myself as the nerdy teenager with a bowl haircut and awful glasses. My low self-esteem and low sense of self-worth drove me, making me feel worthless. Whenever I got in trouble—which was frequently—my adoptive parents would threaten to send me back to Korea. I still remembered what it felt like to live on the streets of Korea not knowing where my next meal was going to come from. So, when my adoptive parents threatened to send me back to Korea, it fueled my internal rage. I was full of hate for my Korean parents, my adoptive parents and toward myself.

As a teenager I was full of angst. I hated everything about myself. I believed that it was me against the world. In talking with other adoptees from Korea and reading their biographies, I've found that many of us had difficult relationships with our adoptive families and ended up either leaving home or being kicked out of the house by the age of seventeen. We struggled to find out what it means to be Korean, how to fit into adoptive countries and cultures and how to find happiness, love and acceptance. This struggle was part of all of us, myself included.

My relationship with my adoptive parents was difficult at best. I had lived on the streets for so long that I continued to steal, scrounge and hoard food. Then my adoptive parents threatened to send me back to Korea, which had a polarizing effect. Instead of scaring me straight, it made me hate them. My Korean parents had abandoned me, and now my adoptive parents were threatening to abandon me. I felt like human garbage—only useful to a point—but then discarded and cast aside once my usefulness was gone.

I hated my Korean parents and had a crappy relationship with my adoptive parents. I started drinking when I was fourteen-years-old, not yet an adult. During my senior year at school, I started having parties at my house and drinking more. I would even go to school and school dances drunk, enraged against the world and my crappy life. I wanted more and I felt that I deserved more.

At age seventeen, I was kicked out of the family home. I was lucky and I had a safety net. My best friend's family took me in and let me live with them. I will never be able to repay the debt that I owe them. After I graduated from high school, I ended up working various minimum wage jobs. I needed to make a change and move out of the city of Westminster, Maryland. Unlike many other Korean adoptees, I took a different path and I enlisted in the United States Marine Corps after high school.

I decided to enlist in the Marine Corps because they were supposed to be the toughest branch. The Marine Corps gave me the discipline and structure I needed. It was physically and emotionally demanding. During the first four years, I was so busy that I didn't have time to get angry or think about anything other than the next training evolution. As an infantryman, someone who is physically on the ground engaging the enemy with weapons fire, securing the key terrain and personnel, my life expectancy in combat was approximately thirty seconds. The statistic aligned perfectly with my self-destructive nature.

The life of an infantryman is not glamorous. We spent an average of four days a week and seven out of eight weeks in the field training for combat. This training might consist of firing various weapons—particularly the Eastern Bloc ones, so we would learn to hear the difference of shots fired from other weapons, identify the type of weapons and be able to pick up and use one of the enemy's guns if need be. We also conducted patrols and night attacks on each other. At other times, we marched up to twenty-five miles, carrying our packs, weapons and full combat load. When my first enlistment approached an end, I decided that I needed to go to college, earn a degree and then gain my commission as a Second Lieutenant in the Marine Corps. I previously dated a lady in New Hampshire and she would urge me to get my degree. Whenever I successfully completed a degree program (either my undergraduate or my two graduate degrees), I would think of her and remember how thankful I should be for pushing me to get a degree.

I have a hard time believing the statistic that only two percent of Americans will serve in the military. The Marines became my family and friends. Most of us volunteered four years of their lives to help defend this great nation and if required, they were prepared to make the ultimate sacrifice—their life. Marines, stereotypically, will sacrifice their lives, not for the nation or the war but for their buddies to their left and right. I re-enlisted and got my commission so that I would make something of myself and continue to pay back a nation that took me in.

I had enlisted into the U. S. Marine Corps as an infantryman—ground troops actual fighting with the enemy. In Infantry Training School, we were told the average life expectancy of each of our different jobs. My job, as a regular infantryman, required no specialized training except fighting and surviving in every climate and place. I decided then not to leave the Marine Corps until I saw combat. But the country was in the cold war with Russia and the Western countries allied against the communist countries. As a result, I never got to test my mettle and see if I would survive the dangers of combat or if I would freeze in fear. I know I would not have frozen in fear because of the Marines in my unit. We would fight for each other, protect each other, risk our lives to save wounded Marines and fight to prove that we were worth the legacy left to us by other Marines—especially those who had fought in previous wars and made the ultimate sacrifice.

Unfortunately, the call to arms didn't come to me until three months after I had left the infantry and one week after Saddam Hussein attacked Kuwait and took over their oilfields. By that time, I was on the commissioning track. Many of us tried to quit the school so we could go back to our units and fight, but we were told that if we quit now we would never have another opportunity to become officers. So we stayed put at the Naval Training Center, attended classes and watched the war play out on television.

The military is indicative of the country from which it came. I worked hard, applied myself diligently and earned each promotion. During my enlisted time in the Marine Corps, I only saw

THE "UNKNOWN" CULTURE CLUB

one other Korean-American. He was in a different company but I made the effort to go over and talk to him. He was adopted like me, had a rough childhood and eventually enlisted in the Marine Corps. As Marines, most of us came from broken families or other difficulties which led us to seek a way out of our respective cities and lives.

While an officer, I met many more Korean-Americans in the Marine Corps especially in California. I was surprised because I had grown up with racism all my life in Maryland. When I was working towards my undergraduate degree at the University of Memphis, I used to play on the Naval Reserve Officer Training Corps' (NROTC) softball tournament held at the Ole Miss University in Mississippi. Memphis was fine in terms of racism as long as you were inside the city limits or in the Eastern suburb called German Town. But the environment was vastly different in Mississippi. When I walked down the street people almost had accidents because they were craning their necks to get a look at me. At the McDonalds, I walked to the counter and proceeded to give the teenager my order. He just stood there for a second and then famously said, "Dang, you speak pretty good. Where you from?"

So how did a Korean-American adoptee end up retiring after twenty-two years of service in the United States Marine Corps? At first it was to prove to myself and the naysayers that I could enlist in the toughest branch of the service and successfully complete boot camp. This led me to reporting to the Infantry Training School (ITS) at Camp Geiger, one of three bases that make up Camp Lejeune in Jacksonville, North Carolina. It was here that I decided not to get out of the Marine Corps until I saw combat. Suddenly and seemingly overnight, I was looking at twenty years in the service. I did everything the hard way: every lesson I learned helped to make me a better person and a better Marine. I often talked to my Marines and used my life as an example of what not to do. Failure was not an option. Not ever.

Growing up as a Korean-adoptee, the last thing I wanted was to be Korean, Asian or different from my friends. I went out of my way to avoid meeting or interacting with other Asians—particularly Koreans. Since the age of six, I had not seen another person of Korean ethnicity. I did everything to ensure that I would not get stationed at Camp Pendleton, a large base in Southern California, housing about 55,000 Marines. Most Marines wanted to transfer to California at some point in their career, but not me. It was easy to remain stationed on the East Coast with few Asians, more racism and very little chance of being deployed to Japan. But when I got into the commissioning pipeline, I had no choice. The school I had to attend was in San Diego, California. When I arrived in May of 1990, I very quickly realized a new feeling: I was no longer the odd duck and I didn't stick out because there were so many Asians.

When I finally did get opportunity to see combat, I was working for the Marine Corps Office of Legislative Affairs (OLA) in the Pentagon. By that time the fighting in Iraq had been in progress for almost two years. The OLA provided support to the Legislative Assistant to the Commandant of the Marine Corps. The Legislative Assistant was normally a one star Brigadier General and the Commandant of the Marine Corps, was head of the service and a Four-Star General. The Legislative Assistant works closely with Congress regarding a multitude of issues from budgeting, buying new weaponry or reviewing complaints by Marines to their Congress person. OLA, like every other office, was tasked with providing Individual Augmentees or volunteers, to go to Iraq and fill positions that had never been staffed or to replace Marines that had to return stateside. By the time I got my orders to go to Iraq, I was a Major with over twenty years of service. I could have retired without ever having to see combat but that was not my goal. I had spent over twenty years of my life preparing to do that which everyone hopes will never come—fight in a war against a common enemy.

I was assigned to Camp Fallujah. Camp Fallujah was staffed and run by Third Country Nationals (TCN) hired by the big Private Military Companies like Kellogg Browning and Root (KBR), Blackwater and others. The TCNs washed our laundry and made our meals. Most of the TCNs were nice people but they were not American and could not really be trusted. Our security forces routinely searched the TCNs quarters and would often find weapons or other things they were prohibited from having.

THE "UNKNOWN" CULTURE CLUB

When I arrived in Iraq, the Iraqi people were preparing for their first national election. As a major I didn't go out on combat patrols or logistics runs. Rather, I was the Protocol Officer for Multi-National Forces West, II Marine Expeditionary Force (Forward). I spent my days in Iraq scheduling, coordinating and conducting visits by Generals, Member of Congress, Secretary of Defense, Secretary of the Navy and even the Secretary of the Air Force. During my seven months in Iraq most of my time was spent coordinating and conducting over one-hundred visits to the Al Anbar Province, home of the Sunnis and home to some of the worst fighting.

While I was standing and waiting at the airstrip for a VIP to fly in, I heard a rocket flying toward me. I immediately ran for cover. Thankfully the rocket impacted far enough away that it didn't do much damage. When the explosion was over, I found myself lying on my back with three herniated discs in my lower back. I didn't want to tell anyone because I felt like it wasn't a real injury given that I didn't get shot or blown up by an Improvised Explosive Device (IED).

In Iraq, I was only able to finagle myself off base on two occasions: the national election in 2005 and then on a flight to Bagdad a few weeks later. The incidents that stand out in my mind are the national election, the missile and the IED that was found on base.

During the national election the streets were closed for all vehicles except coalition vehicles. Once we got away from the base we could see the countryside. It was a bit surreal. Even though we were in the fertile crescent (Nile River valley) there was not much vegetation. There were no vehicles on the road and it all felt so ominous. I had never seen a town after a couple of sieges. All the buildings had holes in them. The space dust like sand covered everything and was ground into everything. Many buildings were either completely destroyed or bore the signs of combat. The Iraqi children we saw playing soccer on the vehicle rides stopped their game and either hid or waited to see what was going to happen next. We were headed to the town center to drop off some Marines for the Security Detail. Once we were in the compound, all we could see were Marines, Iraqi Police and

Iraqi army officials. Once we were safely (no fortified walls) inside, we passed the broken burned out hulk of a destroyed truck.

At the Pentagon, one of my jobs was to track Marines that had been killed in action. I would make sure that the Casualty Affairs Coordination Officer (CACO) for each unit affected had notified the next of kin for each Marine killed in action. I remember the incident which involved the blown up truck. The truck was part of a convoy heading back to base and the passengers were mostly female Marines whose task was to frisk Iraqi women so we did not offend the Iraqis and their families. A Vehicle-Borne Improvised Explosive Device (VBIED) pulled alongside the truck load of female Marines and detonated their explosives. Almost all of the Marines were killed. It was one thing to sit in the Pentagon, reading casualty reports and coordinating efforts to notify next of kin and another thing entirely to see firsthand the damage inflicted by the VBIED. We soon headed back to the base, Camp Fallujah, without any incidents. The elections went well despite Al Quaeda in Iraq's threat of violence.

As the Protocol Officer, I coordinated VIP visits. I was responsible for the Joint Visitors Bureau within Camp Fallujah. The quarters were spacious but not luxurious. And the staff for the visiting dignitary often slept in one or two big rooms with lots of cots in them. Showers were taken in these specifically built trailers. It was nice to be able to get a hot shower and wash the day's worth of sand off. There were periods when the water supply did not function properly and we were placed on water hours, which meant we had very few opportunities to take a shower, maybe an hour or two a day. Some days there simply were no showers.

Part of the routine required me to drive to the airfield, a more remote location on base, at various times of the day or night, usually alone. On some occasions, I would drive as fast as I could through the sand-filled road leading to the airfield to try to stir up a big cloud of sand and make the rear end of the pick-up fish tail. I remember hearing one day that an IED had been found on the road to the airfield. I was shocked. After having been in Iraq and experiencing the booming explosions of outgoing artillery fire, hearing nightly helicopters fly overhead, making hundreds of trips back and forth to the airfield, I knew that Helos during the day usually meant Marines had been hurt and were being transported to the hospital. I had become hardened to the dangers that we faced each day. Who knew if the Sunnis or Al Queda in Iraq would successfully fire off a few rockets at the base? Death could come at such a random time. I drove more carefully after that and I remembered to be constantly aware of my surroundings.

My experience in the Marine Corps and in combat are not meant to take up my full story. I was an orphan that lived on the streets, was then picked up and placed in an orphanage and then a foster home. I was adopted to the US and I had a hard time growing up as a minority. But, I believe my adoptive parents definitely saved me from an early untimely death. They took me in, fed me, gave me clothes and shoes and let me sleep in a bed. For all of their generosity, I hated them and challenged their rules at every opportunity. I would often daydream that my Korean parents would find me and that they would be rich. What I forget was that family was so important to the Korean society. If I had not been adopted abroad, chances are I would have stayed in the orphanage until I could start working.

As a Korean adopted to the US, I grew up as a twinkie: yellow on the outside but white on the inside. I had no idea what Korea was or what it meant to be a Korean. My first experience with Korean food was in high school. I had started working in restaurants when I was 14 and I helped to prepare the family meals. So I thought I could succeed at making kimchee. My parents were away for the weekend and I found a recipe for kimchee and decided to make a batch. I substituted jalapeno peppers for the Korean go chu, red spicy peppers. I was sweating while cutting up the jalapenos and I tried to wipe the sweat from my eye. Big mistake. I got jalapeno pepper juice in my eye and it felt as though I had stuck a white hot poker in my eye. It must have been an hour or two of splashing cold water in my eye before the burning finally stopped. I finally finished the recipe and proudly placed it in the refrigerator. When my adoptive parents arrived home after their weekend trip, they found the kimchee in the refrigerator. I got into more trouble because I stunk up the refrigerator and ruined one of my adoptive mother's favorite plastic containers.

Korean Adoptees, Then and Now

My next encounter with Korean food was in the late 1980s when I was stationed at Camp Lejeune. There was a Chinese restaurant that my Marine buddies and I would go to. The restaurant was owned and run by some Koreans. Their menu had a small section of the menu that listed Korean food. I was intrigued and I ordered *japchae*, clear rice noodles with beef and vegetables. I also tried some of the *jjigae* stews or soups and I was hooked. One of my buddies, Reuben DelValle, and I would go there almost every weekend. On Thursday nights after returning from the field, cleaning everything up, putting everything away and organizing our rooms, we would rush out to the Korean restaurant. Some nights we would get to the restaurant after closing but we would knock on the door anyway and they would let us in and cook for us.

The first time I had time-off at Camp Lejeune or what's called Liberty, was in 1985 when I was a nineteen-years-old and still a slick sleeve private with no rank insignia. When I returned to Camp Lejeune in 1987, the city was pretty much the same. Court Street was where all of the Marines hung out, drank, fought and often got killed. The seedier spots of Jacksonville seemed to be filled with rows of alternating strip bars, pawn shops and tattoo parlors. The strange part was that the majority of the strippers were Koreans. There were actually a lot more Koreans in Jacksonville, North Carolina at that time. The next time I returned to Camp Lejeune was in 1996. By this time Court Street had been cleaned up. There were no more pawn shops nor tattoo parlors. Instead of being everywhere, you had to go looking for them.

The Marine Corps gave me the discipline I lacked as a child—not that my adoptive parents didn't try to teach it. In the Corps, I found other kids like myself, not sure what we were going to do, but ready to serve our country. I had tried to follow my brother into the Maryland State Police but I couldn't make the minimum weight, therefore enlisting in the Marine Corps gave me an alternative. My enlistment was only supposed to be four years but I always wanted to do one more tour, one more duty station, or one more promotion and then, somehow, I found myself after twenty-two years, ready to retire. The Marine Corps filled a void in my life; the discipline and structure replaced what I refused to accept from my parents, and the other Marines became my brothers and sisters. We came from different backgrounds but it didn't matter because our common bond was that we were and will always be Marines.

Why is my story important? I am an orphan, an adoptee, a teenager full of angst, a Marine bent on self-destruction and now a service-disabled veteran. We all share the same struggles: low self-esteem, poor self-worth, fear of rejection and abandonment, as well as trying to figure out who we are, what it means to be Korean and how we fit into the varying adoptive cultures of the countries we had been sent to. I want other orphans and adoptees to know that they are not alone.

✈ **DAVID HAN**
HAN BYUNG HOON

5

DEPORTED

My American name is Monte Haines and my Korean name is Han Ho Kyu. At age eight, I arrived in Iowa almost 6500 miles from Seoul, South Korea. Long golden cornfields, woodlands of elm and hickory covered this earthly terrain. Basement ramblers strewn about vacant neighborhoods fronted by freshly mowed lawns thanks to John Deere tractors, replacing South Korea's city cemented streets—streets I had been used to roaming. I felt like I was left stranded in the middle of a foreign land. I was scared and had no idea where I was.

From the agency, employees sent me to my first adoptive family: Mr. and Mrs. Hormmans, a white couple with two older boys. The whole family had various color of hair just like the land's earthy terrain. One of my first memories is the way everyone stared at me when I arrived. They just kept looking at me strangely.

I was given a small room to sleep in and all went pretty well for the next couple of months, despite the language barrier. Then it started: the physical, mental and sexual abuses. This went on for about six months to a year. My adoptive father used to hit me if I didn't do what he wanted. I attended school with black and blue bruises on my arms and my back. If anyone asked what had happened, I claimed I had fallen down the stairs to protect my adoptive father from getting into trouble.

Sometimes my adoptive father locked me in the closet without food and water. They left me there all day—sometimes for many days. On some bone-chilly Iowan winter days, they made me undress and sent me outside completely naked, tied my hands and feet to two trees and hollered for their two black Doberman Pinschers to nip at my legs as punishment or they shouted for the dogs to chase me around the house. When I came home late from school one day, my dad yanked my right foot and broke one of my toes as punishment. This abuse persisted until a teacher called the Child Protection Agency to investigate the family. Authorities removed me from my adoptive parents' home and sent me to foster care.

I stayed in five different foster homes. The living quarters were crowded and I mostly slept on the floor. I felt like tossed around garbage—like they didn't want me at all. I hid in inconspicuous spaces and remained out of sight for as long as I could. Eventually, the social workers found a family who wanted to adopt me but they weren't allowed because they had too many kids, including a son named Monte. I did stay at the house for a while but I was eventually sent to another foster family.

July of 1981, Holt International Children Services sent me to Mr. and Mrs. Haines. At the age of eleven, I stood in front of a judge and was legally adopted by them. I gained an adoptive brother named John, who was five years older than I, and like a real brother, we did everything together. We formed a real friendship. I assumed that this family would be good for me. I finally found a family who wanted me and I was happy.

My assumption of the happily-ever-after adoption disappeared when I attended school. The students called me names and made fun of me. I ran out of the building and found a place to hide. While crying, I thought, what did I do wrong? Why am I so different from the other kids?

During the summer, my nightmare came back to haunt me. Mr. Haines, my new adopted father, a man with a good reputation within the community, abused me physically, mentally and sexually. After coming home from playing outside, my dad hit me with a bread board so hard that I blacked out. Other times my dad crept in my room at night and crawled into bed with me. I endured this for a long time. He also abused my older adopted brother.

My dad kicked my brother out of the house when he was sixteen-years-old and I didn't get to see him for a very long time. I was only eleven at the time and now the only child left in the household. As a consequence, all the abuse was then focused on me. My mom was too scared to leave or to call the cops. If I didn't mow the lawn, rake the grass and other chores correctly, my adoptive father would slam my head against a concrete wall. This seemed to go on all the time. My mom couldn't handle the abuse and finally divorced him.

My adoptive father moved me and himself to Colorado, along with a friend of mine and his mom, who moved in with us. It seemed like the living conditions were going well until one day a police officer pulled me from class and told me that my dad was arrested for child abuse against my friend and me. My friend's mom called the cops.

I had to leave Colorado to live with my adoptive mom. I didn't get along with her very well due to being previously abandoned by her but she treated me better than my father did. I ran away from home and headed for the airport, trying to go back home to Korea where I belonged.

After I graduated from high school, I enlisted in the United States Army. Because the military enlistment did not require proof of US citizenship, I never doubted my status as a US citizen. I served in the Gulf War for three and a half years and lost many friends there. When I returned to civilian life, it was hard for me to sleep at night. I woke from nightmares and I couldn't forget the images of war. Some people call this Gulf War Syndrome or Post Traumatic Stress Disorder.

After the military, I found a job as a truck driver. On February 27, 2001, my driving partner and I were assigned to take a load to the East Coast. When I came to the check point, the authorities were waiting for us. My driving partner didn't tell me he had planted drugs in the truck's trailer.

Korean Adoptees, Then and Now

I spent my time in a jail cell where I was locked up full-time, in a prison, and also in an immigration-holding detention center. Inside, there seemed to be around thirty Korean adoptees at the risk of being deported. I learned later that every state has these detention centers. In each one of these, you'll find ten to twenty Korean adoptees, standing by to be deported back to Korea.

My older brother, John, and I fought my case to the best of our ability and to the point of exhaustion from explaining my defense. Eventually, I gave up hope and told him to stop helping me. I knew it was a lost cause.

On December 25th, 2005, I was released on house arrest and required to report monthly to the US Immigration and Customs Enforcement (ICE), a Department of Homeland Security. I was required to go to Houston, Texas where the Korean consul was located in order to obtain a passport. There, I was not allowed to leave the state. I was told my name was not recorded in their computer.

"What?!" I was shocked. "Why not?"

"Your situation is kind of strange to us," the man from the Immigration Office told me.

I asked again, "Why?"

"You're adopted, but you're not a US citizen," he said.

Completely shocked, I was like, "I am a US citizen. I was adopted in '81. The law says if you're adopted by an American citizen, you are an American US citizen." During my visit, I asked, "Why can't you help me?"

His only response was that he was afraid of Homeland Security.

I went back to my American home empty-handed and lived out of my car. Fortunately, I found a job with a construction company and reported regularly into the ICE office while applying for a passport to Korea.

My older brother, John, killed himself with a shotgun on August 20, 2008. The trauma for me was unbearable and I didn't report into ICE that month as required. When an immigration officer called me, I simply stated, "I didn't report because my brother died."

THE "UNKNOWN" CULTURE CLUB

Only two months later, officers in full SWAT uniforms barged into my room—a garage turned into a living space—pointing handguns and M16 assault rifles at me while shouting, "Get on the ground!" as if I had been a convicted terrorist. They pushed my knees onto the floor, handcuffed my wrists together and ushered me back to a detention center. I was accused of threatening a deportation officer but they didn't believe me when I told them this was not true. Instead, I was thrown back into a cell, with the door locked behind me.

When I stood in front of the Immigration Judge, he scolded: "You are not allowed in *my* country. This is *my* country. This is *my* land. I want you out of it."

On November 4, 2009, I was deported back to Korea wearing only jeans and a T-shirt. I had only twenty dollars on me, I couldn't speak the language and I didn't know where to go. All forms of my identification and personal documents were confiscated. My escorts, four men and one woman dressed in civilian clothes, basically dropped me off at the Incheon Airport and left me there on the grey tarmac more than six thousand miles away from everything I knew for almost forty years. Forever gone were the strewn-about basement ramblers, long golden cornfields, woodlands of elm and hickory. Rather, South Korea's city cemented streets—streets I would roam as a homeless person—replaced the John Deere tractor-mowed lawns. Grey low winter clouds chilled me to the bone. Again, I felt stranded in a foreign land. No longer able to speak the Korean language, I was scared and had no idea where to go.

✈ **MONTE HAINE**

6

BEHIND THE SMILE

The first photo probably ever taken of me is sitting on the lap of a young girl holding my "orphanage" identification number and a "given" birth date. Yep, when The Who sang, "I'm not a Number," it was not true for me. I started out as Soon Ok Wang, born May 31, 1960, #3564.

Now, I know you're probably already thinking, oh, what a lovely story this is going to be. When I meet people for the first time, questions just pour out. Many of us are interested in knowing other people's past—especially if they are another ethnicity. But, back in the 60s and 70s, it was especially fascinating to know someone who wasn't born in the United States. Now, it's actually common to meet someone from another country. God bless our potpourri of origins.

The plain fact is I hate meeting new people. A typical conversation goes: "Where are you from?" Or, downright rude people might ask: "Wad are you?" I answer: "I'm Korean." They ask: "Were you born here?" I say: "No, I was adopted when I was three-years-old." They exclaim, "Oh, wow. That is wonderful. You must be very grateful!" I cringe.

I was diagnosed with a congenital right hip, and polio in my left leg. I have a scar on my left hip, and a scar down my upper left leg, traces of surgery. For a while I wore a full body cast. I would love for a doctor to read my records and tell me in layman's terms all the crap that was done to me. I'm glad I was too young to remember all that because it sounds too painful. I was once told that I made medical history because it had been assumed that I would never walk.

Being diagnosed with polio, and after my first surgery, I was able to take my first step at the age of four. There would be three more surgeries. The polio had taken about 50% of the upper muscle in my left leg so it left me with a strut, so to speak. Most people don't even know I have a handicap until they see me walking.

The things that most people take for granted, like walking without pain, running, skipping. God, I would love to skip, squat, climb stairs without using a handrail or buy shoes in adult sizes. Simple shit like that.

But most devastatingly, polio robbed me of fun. I can't roller skate, ice skate, ski and, most of all, I can't dance. I can dance rock and roll style but I can't do structured-type dancing. I would love to just line-dance, salsa, waltz, or hell—even polka! In my dreams I can do all this stuff, but then I wake. *It sucks.*

Don't get me wrong, I'm grateful I can even walk and, yes, there are many even more unfortunate ones with polio and other handicaps, but it wouldn't be normal for me not to be resentful that life seemed to cut me a bad hand. The only consolation that I give myself is that I always say: "In my next life, I will do all these and much more."

An early memory I have while in Korea is laying on a rolling board low to the ground after the first surgery. I suspect that that was the way I got around. Okay, who can say they remember something like that?

I remember being put in some really hot water and crying, possibly screaming. I was at the doctor's office and for whatever reason they placed me in hot water. I suppose it was some kind of water therapy, but WTF?!

THE "UNKNOWN" CULTURE CLUB

I have a photo of me resting on Grandma Holt's lap and looking up at her. I love the way we're gazing into each other's eyes. I must have felt her kindness—something that would be foreign to me in my youth. It calms me just looking at this picture to know that I had glimpses of goodness.

I was one of three girls sent to a white couple (Connie and Joseph), who were in their late 50s, and decided to start a second family through Holt International Children Services. Both had been previously married, and each had two grown children. They adopted my first sister in 1959 at the age of three, my second sister in 1960 at the age of two, and I was added in 1963, at the age of three. I was not the intended adoptee when Connie and Joseph flew overseas to Korea in 1963. The girl they were going to adopt had tuberculosis, so it was divine intervention that they picked me. I had something wrong with my leg but I was good to go, so off I went to America.

I have such fond memories of my adoptive daddy, Joseph William Adams. My memories are brief and few, but they live long after he passed in 1972. I remember riding on his shoulders. He was so tall, over six feet, that I felt like I was up in the sky. I think I wrote one time when I was young that he was as tall as a giraffe. I loved when he held my hand cause his were so big and warm. The best memories were when he would dry my hair with the towel. He rubbed my head so gently and it felt so warm and comfortable just sitting there letting him massage my scalp.

The best-captured picture I have of my daddy was when he taught me to ride a tricycle. One photo, in particular, radiated his gentleness as he bent down to check the placement of my feet on the pedals.

Around the age of five, when I finally was able to walk, I would race my daddy down the street while he drove a green work truck that had green wooden flat bed gates latched on by hinge locks. He would sometimes come home for lunch and upon leaving, he would drive slowly down the block so I could "race" him to the corner. He always let me win.

When just my sisters and I rode with him on Sunday's, Dad would let us stop at the store and buy candy—our little secret from our adoptive mother. Oh, how I wish I could remember more of the little things I did with him. I'm sure they were always calm and possibly magical. But in short, I just remember him as always being kind.

He would sit in the backyard and brush our two Samoan dogs, Crystal and Star, beautiful white fluffy dogs with the sweetest eyes and white lashes. He was always in the backyard—probably by choice but truthfully, he was not allowed in the house unless it was dinner time or he was doing the dishes.

I never knew what he did all that time in the backyard and garage but I remember finding in his tool box a small whistle that had been whittled from wood. I wished I had kept it. The only thing I have in his memory is his Westclox watch, which continues to be enough because it keeps on ticking! I wound it up and it still works! Now if you're doing the math, this watch hasn't run for forty years. This must be my daddy's way of letting me know he is still running in my heart.

The first time I ever truly cried from sadness was when he was in the hospital. Connie, my adoptive mom, always told my sisters and me, that he was illiterate and stupid. Those were her fond words describing him. Anyway, he was dying of cancer and it was the one and only time I saw him in the hospital. He had the Bible in his lap and was reading "The Lord is my Shepherd" and then he lifted his head and recited the rest of the passage. My eyes watered and tears ran down my face. I had to leave the room because I didn't want to show my emotions.

At his funeral, I was in a daze, and remember seeing his body. I remember a lot of people were there and some people were speaking of him with such loving, kind memories. I realized then, he was a well-loved man, and I regretted that I never got to really know him as much as I wanted. I was twelve when he died and was old enough to know that I could and should have had a relationship with him but I was never allowed to.

I remember when I felt my heart truly break for the first time, about a year after he died. We were cleaning out his stuff in his bedroom, when I opened the bottom drawer to find it full of empty Bufferin bottles. It dawned on me that he must have been hiding excruciating pain for many months, perhaps years. One day I just broke down in hysterical crying—gut wrenching fetal-position crying. I felt my heart literally splitting in two, and realized that this was what a broken heart feels like. However, the sweet memories that I do have will last until we can meet again.

The only good memory I have of Connie, my adoptive mother, is the song she would sing at breakfast time: "Patty's going to walk to school. Tra la la la..." That's it! I try to muster up some sort of goodness for her, but nothing comes.

My earliest memories of Connie's abuse include being flung from one end of the room to the other, getting rug burns, hair pulled, head banged against the wall, and constantly being slapped in the face. This is what I remember of my adoptive mother.

Yes, to say the least, she was enraged—a rager. And she took out her rage on the children! Bi-Polar wasn't diagnosed in the 1960s and 70s. Common sense now tells that she had anger issues. Yes, I'm sure she must have suffered tragic incidents in her early life, but her actions seemed vengeful especially since I was a mere child. She even beat me while I was still in my body cast at the age of four.

Beginning early on in our adoption, Connie used to spit in our faces and scold my sisters and me that she would pack our bags and send us back to Korea to be the sluts, whores, and slanted-eyed monsters that we were. Her additional personal touch for my case was that since I was a "crippled idiot," no one would want me as a whore, so I'd probably die on the streets. As we got older, her wrath against us included the word cunt. I didn't know what this word meant at the time, but just the sound of it, I knew the word was filthy. This was usually our Sunday morning gospel speech before we attended Sunday School and repented for being the sluts, whores and slanted-eyed monsters we were accused of being.

I cried during this time, which would lead my adoptive mother to scold, "Stop that crying." After slapping us, she would then threaten like in all good psychotic parenting, "Or I'll give you a reason to cry!" An epiphany came years later and I said to myself, go ahead and pack my f**king bags and send me back to f**king Korea. It can't be any worse than here.

Korean Adoptees, Then and Now

What became an outlet for me? Cussing! I remember uttering the words, Jesus Christ. God, that felt f**king good. But I wasn't smart enough to keep it to myself. Somehow, the cuss words slipped out and Connie overheard. When a bar of ivory soap is scraped along the upper teeth and then held there, I didn't know it would burn and make me want to throw up.

To this day, I have a real potty mouth. My language has toned down but I still find myself thinking, oh, I did it again. Besides verbal obscenities, I took kindly to the visual of "flipping the bird," a feel-good hand gesture. However, that got me into trouble, too. My sister, whether deliberately or just because she decided to, shouted, "why'd you flip her off?" Her question was cause enough to motivate my adoptive mother into using the bottom dull end of a silverware knife and slamming it into my finger, careful not to leave telltale evidence of physical abuse.

Another time my adoptive mother got really mad at me for losing my door key. She had a thing about keys, I guess. This wasn't the usual anger though. Her rage went on for days possibly weeks. Her initial anger was so intense that she actually bit one of my ears after screaming into them.

Mornings seemed to be her raging time. She would give her rants and raves and then if there was food conveniently at hand she would smash toast in our faces and, of course, the hot oatmeal was always the special touch. She used to cook eggs in a double boiler steamer and then throw the hot watery eggs at us. Her cooking was atrocious.

My sisters and I each had our least favorites so we would bargain with each other for the least of the worse. Some days I would have all grapefruit while someone choked down the watery eggs or lumpy oatmeal. Dinners were no better. I hated peas. Still do unless they're mixed in with other veggies. One night, I tried to hide the peas in my apron. Yes, we had to wear aprons for every meal. All I remember is sitting there almost all night. I don't even remember what happened after that but I must have had to have eaten them or I'd still be sitting there.

My adoptive mother suffered from migraines and when she would go hiding into her room for days, her absence became a great relief. The fear awoke when she eventually emerged. We

THE "UNKNOWN" CULTURE CLUB

never knew who was going emerge from that room. My sisters and I would try to be quiet but god forbid if we weren't, she would exit and Satan would be present.

During these times we could identify with a Mommy Dearest type of midnight madness, most frequent during her migraine episodes. In the middle of the night she made us stand in the hallway for who knows what reason. She would drag me out of bed and command, "Go to the bathroom," and "do not get up until you're done." So there I sat too afraid to get up. Many a night, I fell asleep on that toilet.

I had acquired a strange little habit, she says from the orphanage of rocking myself to sleep. I would rock my head back and forth to get myself tired. Well, that was just too weird for her so when she would catch me doing it, into the hallway she'd make me stand. God forbid if I wet the bed which I did a couple of times. That required a slap session, head bangs and more standing in the hallway.

The only time I ever remember her being "remorseful" was when she spanked me on my ass with the bristles of a brush. It left pinhole marks with a bit of bleeding. She rubbed some ointment on it but she never said sorry. I knew that she knew she had broke her code of leaving marks on us.

Sometimes she would do the conventional beatings. Switches from a branch that we would have to pick ourselves, or paddles from that paddle/ball toy.

She was very clever that way. Slaps left red marks but never bruises or black eyes. When I had braces though, I remember many times my lips were cut on the insides. Pulling our hair wasn't visible either. Boxing of the ears just left ringing. Rugs burns on knees and elbows, too many to count but still easily explained. Banging our heads against the wall was her favorite though—she was literally trying to knock sense into us. There were so many knots on my head, sometimes multiple but it always seemed I would just be getting over one and BAM, a new one.

One visible mark she did leave was a huge blister on my finger from being thrown against the furnace. I was late to school that day and I recall someone in the office asking me how I got that red face? I, of course, claimed to have fallen but I think the school employee suspected differently probably because my face was still red from being slapped.

Then came the day when Connie got careless. My nieces and nephews and some neighbor friends were over at the house. Calla was practicing the piano and made some mistake. My adoptive mother told me to give her the hammer but I think I ended up giving her a nutcracker. She hit Calla on the head with it and the yellow sweater she was wearing started showing red. My adoptive mother took Calla to the doctors and made some lame excuse, but after that Calla was never the same. She started having blackouts and was put on Dilantin for seizures. After that more heavy medications that doctors used back in the 70s and it was the beginning of Calla's medication struggles. Calla had longed to be a nurse but her physical and emotional problems never allowed her to be that bright, inspired woman she was meant to be.

Now this abuse wasn't exclusive to us girls. There were many altercations between my adoptive parents, with her usually being the provoker. Cops were called several times and I remember my adoptive dad leaving a few times, but he always came back. There were only a few times that I witnessed him being really angry. He put his fist through the door a couple of times and then he would have to fix the door.

The one time I remember that he was a real man was when she threw a plate at him. He came storming out of the kitchen with the plate in his hand. She crawled under the table right by me, so he kicked her in the ass. It's about time, I thought. I was so proud of him.

During this time I was doing somewhat okay in school, getting all As, but something started changing: I couldn't focus or remember things. The trauma from the abuse was taking its toll. By the time I got to sixth grade my attention span was nil, probably around my adoptive daddy's death and because I had missed some school. I couldn't grasp math at all and the teachers either didn't pay attention or care. I couldn't do even simple math in my head yet today I'm a bookkeeper. Go figure. Give me a calculator, excel spreadsheets and I'm a whiz but to do math in my head, not possible. Reading comprehension and retention is very diffi-

THE "UNKNOWN" CULTURE CLUB

cult yet I do enjoy reading even though I can't remember much. Now that may be true for a lot of people, but I pretty much know how mine came about.

Around the time I was about eight we had been going to music lessons from a man who had been teaching us since I was four years old. We three girls were my adoptive mother's "Little Trio Singing Angels."

Our male teacher was kind to us, even taking us for ice cream and talking with us. He even let us talk kind of naughty. I don't remember what, but it was stuff we definitely weren't allowed to say at home. He gained our trust and you could say love. Any kind of attention from him was good attention.

Every week we had our lessons, but one particular day he put his hand up my shirt and asked me if it felt good. I knew this was terribly wrong so I told my sisters in the car while my adoptive mother was still inside probably paying him for his hard earned time. They both were pissed because needless to say they had been going through the same thing for years and now for him to be doing this to me was the last straw. So thinking this was the something we should tell an adult, we told our adoptive mother. All hell broke loose. He was fired immediately. Later it was discovered that we had not been the only ones.

I finally retaliated. I was vacuuming one day and my adoptive mother was just about to slap me. I picked up the vacuum and slammed it down and looked straight into her face and said "Don't you dare." The fearful look in her eyes was priceless.

I ran away at the age of seventeen and ¾ years. I had two months of fear that she would find me and throw me in juvenile detention but I think she finally figured out that I wasn't coming back willingly so she let it go. The last time she was ever a part of my life, she had come over to my new apartment and proceeded to tell me how I was going to hell because I didn't have a picture of Jesus up on the wall. I politely told her that it was time for her to leave and she never saw me alone again, only at family functions.

There were so many times I had envisioned tying my adoptive mother in a chair, slapping her and spewing out all the venom I had in me but my way was even better. She never saw my daughter and died knowing that she never would. That was my way of showing my appreciation for all her love and nurturing. To be loved is to give love.

I drowned out my past with drugs and alcohol and have crossed over that invisible line of no return. For over thirty years I numbed myself with no solutions of how to live life without that pain, shame, guilt, and hatred in my heart. When it all came to a crash after my marriage fell apart and my life had no meaning, I tried to end it all. I was so tired of being sick and tired. I was tired of meeting people and coming to the crossroad of truth or fantasy.

I had to make a decision: do I die an alcoholic or do I live as a sober woman?

I live today with a spiritual purpose that my story is not tragic; in fact, many people I have met are adopted, abused, physically challenged and yet our stories are our strengths and hopes for others. I have solutions today for living a beautiful life that's filled with honesty, compassion and love.

I never really thought about being adopted. It was just a fact and besides, my sisters were also Asian adoptees so it was always known. I don't believe I ever had an abandonment issue but I do remember holding my infant daughter who was crying in my arms. I broke down crying because I wondered who held me when I was an infant, who soothed me when I was crying. I may never know but I realized at that moment that my daughter was my flesh and blood and that we were the beginning of a whole new generation. And if she never has children, I am content to know that it is the two of us that were bonded in love and we existed.

I have recently joined some Facebook Korean Adoptees KAD groups. I have met one woman from my early years of the 1960s and met another KAD who flew over on the same flight in November of 1963. I have no expectations of ever finding my Korean family but I have family that goes beyond blood; they are my heart and soul. I have loved and been loved. That is my journey.

✈ **KELLI BUHR**

SECTION TWO:

"UNKNOWN" CULTURE

7

THE BLIND GIRL

I'm fuzzy on the details. I'm not even exactly sure of the year, but I do recall the essential elements of this story with clarity. The emotions are crystal clear. I think it was the summer of 1976, returning home from a South Korean "motherland" trip, I discovered a mysterious and unexplainable truth about love and connection.

In that summer, as a Korean-born adoptee, I had the opportunity to return to Korea as a young adult. I was mildly curious about my birth country and the cost of this organized tour of Korea was very reasonable. The airfare was made affordable due in part to the fact that I would be escorting newly adopted children back to the United States to be delivered to their new families. Escorting the children meant that I would be responsible for their safety and well-being on the transpacific flight. Because of this, flight attendants would not be required to spend as much time with the Korean children assigned to adoptive and waiting families, and would be free to attend to usual and customary on-flight duties. I didn't receive any special training, other than an hour or so of instructions.

Korean Adoptees, Then and Now

This briefing included how to strap the children into their seats by using pillows as braces, how to take the children's outer garments off to keep them clean, and then redress them before landing to make them look nice for their new American parents—all who had never seen their new child in person. Strict instructions were given, one of which was to avoid feeding the children any western food on the airlines. It was explained that the children's digestive system would not be accustomed to the rich food, which could lead to diarrhea on a long flight—something to be avoided at all costs.

During the motherland tour, we spent nearly two weeks traveling the full length of South Korea. For part of the trip we stayed in peoples' homes. For a few nights we stayed in the orphanage that I had lived in as a toddler. The remainder of the trip we traveled and took in the sights. We ate great food and saw national landmarks and tourist locations. At the end of the two weeks we were given the instructions on how to escort the children.

Then, at the offices of Holt Korea, foster mothers brought the young children for the big trip. The children were a mix of infants and toddlers with an older child or two included. The social workers reviewed photo albums of the new families with the children old enough to understand. In a few minutes their entire world would change. The children would be placed on an airplane and the predominant language would instantly change from Korean to English. Instead of squat toilets they would be expected to use western toilets. Instead of chopsticks, they would use fork and knives. And instead of sleeping on floor mats, they would sleep atop a mattress on a raised bed.

I was assigned three children: two boys, approximately two-years-old; and a girl, approximately five-years-old. The boys were excited and wound-up. The girl was afraid, crying, withdrawn and blind.

The first step of the journey consisted of going through the departure gate and onto the airplane. Although social workers accompanied us part of the way through the process, at a certain point they were not allowed to go further. I was on my own. I escorted the three children, shuffling with their bags, their official papers, and tried to carry my own bags and documents, while fumbling our way through the airport. The boys were eager with big eyes. The blind girl was terrified and cried constantly—her body trembling. There was nothing I could do to get her to stop from being afraid.

When we finally made it onto the airplane I tried to talk to the little girl, but I spoke in English and the more I spoke the louder she cried. I tried to touch her but she recoiled and cried louder. It seemed that her crying become softer when I left her alone.

The eight-hour flight took off from Seoul, South Korea and headed toward Anchorage, Alaska. When the plane pulled away from the terminal the boys became fearful too. Eventually, they quietly fell asleep after we became airborne, but the little blind girl continued to cry and moan. I was nervous and tried to comfort her, but nothing worked. I am sure she must have fallen asleep some time during the flight—but I just do not remember that happening. It seemed that she cried and sobbed for the entire flight.

Throughout the long night flight, I could not help but wonder who would adopt this little blind girl: *Doesn't everyone want a perfect baby? Doesn't everyone want a child that is developmentally normal? And considered beautiful? Who would want to adopt an imperfect girl without sight? What was the motivation?* But I was looking at this little girl through the lens of my eyes and my life expectations. I marveled at the thought that this crying blind girl was going to a family in the United States. Who were they exactly?

Our port of entry to the United States was Anchorage, Alaska and the children and I were met at the airport by Holt volunteers who would help them through customs. The volunteers fed and played with them, giving me a small break and the ability to get through customs on my own. I was already tired and I would be continuing on to New York.

One of the escorts took the boys to a different destination in the United States and I continued assisting the blind girl to New York City. The little girl was tired too, but she was more afraid and continued sobbing. Again, I assume looking back, that she must have slept for part of the trip. It just seemed that she was constantly either quietly weeping or sobbing for the entire flight. By the time we arrived at the airport in New York I was exhausted. I was not used to being around young children, and I felt the pressure of being responsible for someone else's child. I also felt the added pressure to keep the peace on the flight for the other passengers. I didn't want the crying to disturb them, and I was self-conscious of their glances at us and curious looks. Escorting was a lot like babysitting in a closet without any lights. On top of all that, the flight was long and being responsible for hours on end became exhausting. From the port of departure, through Anchorage customs and then onto New York took nearly twenty-four hours!

In New York we were again met by Holt volunteers. Their job was to take the little girl and present her to the new waiting family. The questions of the last hours weighed heavily on me, and I wanted to see who would be adopting this very scared, trembling blind girl. Who was going to be her new parents?

At JFK Airport in New York, a volunteer ushered the weeping girl off the plane. It took me a few minutes to gather my own things and exit the plane but I hurried to follow the two who by then had disappeared around a corner. As I turned the bend, I saw the volunteer hand the girl over to a sighted woman and to a blind man. As the small group huddled tightly together the world stopped and became silent. The blind man touched the face of the little girl with his hand—his new daughter—and she reached up and touched his face. As the two connected, she stopped sobbing and became relaxed and calm, the first time in nearly twenty-four hours. The connection was instantaneous and the love miraculous.

✈ **BLAIR KING**

8

FINDING A FAMILY

May 22, 1984. According to our adoption records this was the date my twin sister and I were found abandoned in front of the Cheongdo-gun district office in North Gyeongbuk Province.

Cheongdo-gun is a small district known for its annual bullfights and persimmon tree-lined streets. The locals claim bragging rights for inspiring the Saemaeul Movement, a public policy considered, by both fans and critics of Park Chung Hee alike, the foundation of the country's lightening-speed economic development. After suffering from a typhoon in 1969, the people in one area of Cheongdo-gun district gathered together to re-tile the towns' roofs and rebuild its roads. As the story goes, Park Chung Hee, on his way to another town to survey the damage incurred from the typhoon, saw them all from his train window, working together, regardless of age or gender, to rebuild the village and had the train stopped. After speaking with the townspeople and hearing that they had all come to a decision to work together to rebuild the town voluntarily, the story goes, Park was inspired to create the Saemaeul Movement, in order to build a spirit of "self-sufficiency" and "cooperation" in farmers and other people in the countryside that he felt was necessary to attain the scale of economic development that he envisioned for the country. He launched the program, aimed at nationwide modernization, the next year in 1970, citing Cheongdo-gun as the model of communities cooperating to self-improve and take care of their own. Or so the story goes.

On the same day we were purportedly found in front of the district office, we were taken to a children's welfare facility in Gyeongsan City, also in North Gyeongbuk Province. The facility that we are reported to have lived for two years is called Sungrakwon. It is now a welfare facility for people with disabilities. In 2007, about six months after coming to Korea and still knowing very little about my past, I mistakenly assumed that the facility was in Daegu, a larger city neighboring Gyeongsan, where my American parents had lived for two years. I went there in April of 2007, hoping to find Sungrakwon but was unsuccessful.

2007.04.22 the first five years

there's something about living abroad that makes you feel like everything is one layer removed from reality. i suppose i'm realizing the irony that on a journey that is supposed to be about learning about myself, i don't feel completely like myself.

i visited daegu, the city where i was born and lived until i was five. the trip was nothing monumental, certainly. that is to say, i didn't have any epiphanies on my life. there were no earth shattering memories that came racing back to me. it was just a town that held significance because i knew that it should. i've been having some trouble finding the orphanage that i lived in but i went to another orphanage in daegu. i spent the afternoon with the children and when i looked at these kids, something intangible inside me sparked. i'm not sure what it was, i can't describe it but it was red. not a bright red, but a deep red and it felt warm and wet and moved like a wave. not a fast wave that crashed quickly in and back out. not a gentle wave that ebbed as slowly as it had rolled in. but one that flooded in quickly and then slowly fell back.

When I was younger I had secretly wished the story of babies being delivered by storks was true, even long after I was old enough to know that it couldn't possibly be. But couldn't it? My life as an American began after being carried over an ocean in the mouth of a stork made of metal and glass.

When I was in seventh grade my English teacher gave my class an assignment to write "A History of Me." The best essays were to be submitted to a nationwide writing contest with the same prompt. Piecing together two facts that I had heard at various time growing up: 1) your father was in a war 2) you were adopted while we lived in Korea and one fact that I had picked up somewhere along the way 3) there was once a war in Korea, I wrote with great gusto a compelling tale about how my dad, bullets whizzing over his head, had survived the war and adopted my sister and me. I learned too late that the war in Korea was in the 1950s. The math would've made me a 45-year old 7th grader. I won honorable mention in the nationwide contest. When my parents read the essay, they laughed at the fact that the historical inaccuracy of my essay had somehow escaped both my English teacher and a panel of judges. My parents told me I could still keep the prize. – a plaque that got hung somewhere in the trophy case at my school and a boxful of books that were shipped to directly to our house. Being a child who loved books, I opened the box with great ceremony. Within the several dozen books was one called *Molly By Any Other Name*, a book about an Asian-American teenager, adopted by a white family, who finds her mother. The book cover had a drawing of an Asian girl on the front. I felt both uncomfortable and drawn to read it at the same time. I read it in one sitting. I felt like I was betraying my parents just by reading it. It felt like a secret. I read the book over and over, but I hid it from my parents. I wondered what great cosmic forces were at work for me to get this book as an award for writing a false history of myself. Maybe the judges had known after all and had taken pity on me, specifically selecting the book and hiding it among the twenty or so others in the box.

I returned to Cheongdo-gun for the first time on October 31st 2008. Halloween. Why did this seem fitting? I felt like I was on a hunt for ghosts. I took the bullet train from Seoul to Daegu with plans to meet a volunteer translator at the East Daegu train station. I had asked my boyfriend at the time if he could get the day off to come with me. He seemed ambivalent. I told him I would be fine going it alone. I think in my heart I never forgave him for it. But in hindsight, I was thankful that he had not come. Completely alone and in front of people who were all seeing me for the first time, I felt something forcing me to remain composed. Without that pressure I might have fallen apart. Keep it together, I kept repeating in my head. But I have had a lifetime of practice at pretending to be strong when I feel my weakest.

   I went with the volunteer first to the district office. The people working there showed me some documents that, even having studying Korean for about a year, had so much *hanja* on them that they meant nothing. The district office worker essentially retraced the steps that I had so far taken in order to find my family. According to our adoption records, my sister and my Korean names were Jung Hana and Jung Doona, meaning first and second. After being found, we were brought to Sungrakwon. Where we lived until we were transferred to Holt two years later in January of 1986. Almost one month later, my American parents walked into the Holt office and expressed their interest in adoption. The problem was Sungrakwon had no records of twins with our names having stayed at their facility. However, they had the records of a pair of sisters, one year apart in age, Jung Namhee and Jung Namjung, who had come from Cheongdo-gun on May 22, 1984. When I first heard this news, via email, I felt the wind knocked out of me. It was possible that Sharon and I were not twins. And the names that we had known all of our lives, one of the few pieces of information that we had believed to be certain (because our records stated that we had self-reported our names), might not be real. The name that I had spent so much of my life feeling awkward and embarrassed about anytime anyone in our family brought up, but that I had finally made my peace with, the one that I had finally started to feel like belonged to me - might not be mine after all. I had been using my Korean name in my Korean classes and the name felt like it fit. In particular, I liked that my name, meaning two, inherently implicated my relationship to my sister, one. I had written a paper that had been accepted for publication and had submitted my name as Shannon Doona Heit. The journal had not yet gone to press and I immediately had the name deleted. I felt like I had been betrayed by this name that I had made significant, that I had allowed myself to try on and wear outside. But here I was again vulnerable and exposed. It was another cruel reminder that I had to depend on others to know even the most basic things about myself.

I dreaded telling my sister the news. I knew especially that the possibility that we might not be twins would devastate her. But I had started this search with the goal of finding the truth. And the truth was what I wanted, no matter how much it hurt to hear. Later, when I told my parents, my mom responded that even if I found out we were not twins, we would always be twins to her. In fact, she said defiantly, she would still tell people we were twins. I became angry, hot faced and I could feel my jaw clench. I asked, *Why would she do that?* If I found out we weren't and she said we were twins in front of me, I would tell people she was lying. She looked like I had slapped her. I was being hurtful but I was angry. Why was I going to all the effort to find out the truth if in the end, they wouldn't even accept it? My dad, feeling the tension, cautiously offered the information that, in fact, they had requested twins and the adoption agency had located twins so quickly that he had always entertained the idea that it was a farce. I wondered, how could they have knowingly engaged with an institution when deep down they had questioned the ethics of it? The office worker explained to me that they had contacted the family of Jung Namhee and Jung Namjung and arranged for me to meet them today. The parents had both already passed away. I would be meeting a cousin and possibly the father's *noona*. As a sidenote he said that there was a Jung Hana and Jung Doona in the Cheongdo-gun records as well. But they were reported to be living happily in Busan.

We took a winding car ride and ended up at a grove filled with trees where people were working. One of the workers met us as we pulled up, an older woman, probably in her late fifties. I was told she was a distant cousin from the father's side of the family. She scanned my face carefully. In that moment, I thought of the time that I had gone with an old boyfriend to track down his father's estranged family in Puerto Rico. He had never met them but I had bought our tickets to Puerto Rico as a graduation present and encouraged him to try to find them. I had stood awkwardly off to the side when, after driving all of over the town in a small rental car, we had finally been led from a funeral home that had been in the family for generations, to his aunt's house. I had found it remarkable,

2006.06.02 tales of puerto rico

i was bearing witness to an intimate moment between two strangers as they searched each other's faces in an attempt to confirm that they did, in fact, belong to each other, somehow.

Four months later I uprooted myself and moved to Korea, under the guise of teaching English, to learn about the country where I had lived until I was five, but had no memories of – except ones that I questioned myself. Were they real? Had I fabricated them in a dream? They felt more like cobwebs than memories, whispers or shadows that could be brushed away with even the slightest gust of wind.

As this woman peered into my face, I caught her eye and I felt like I was pleading with her but I had no idea for what. Maybe I was pleading for her to restore my memory. Yes, she finally announced, she kind of looks like so-and-so, who was so-and-so's daughter. Yes, yes, definitely. She looks exactly like so-and-so. Exactly. We went back to her house. Her entire neighborhood felt covered with a canopy of persimmon trees and the fruit was in season. In her house there were bowls and bowls of the husky fruit spilling out on every surface. On the counters, on the shelves, on the tables, on the floor, even. She selected some of the largest, ripest persimmons and pulling out a knife from her pocket, she sliced them for me on the spot. She put the fruit in my mouth, fed me by hand, asking me if I liked the taste. It felt like she was asking if I was one of them. She called other relatives and suddenly there was a group of people peering curiously at me, taking in every last detail of my face, my hands, my feet. One relative remarked that my feet looked exactly like so-and-so. Just look at her feet! Without a doubt, so-and-so's feet. It was settled,

I was told that we were going to a *haniwon* where the father's sister was getting some treatment.

When I met the aunt, she was immediately certain. She looked at me in a way that was almost hungry, a way that made me feel embarrassed but also good. She was absolutely certain. I was the daughter of her brother who had passed away some twenty-odd years before. She held my hand and stroked it and she made me promise to come back. She gave me her phone number and made me promise to call her and she said once more, to come back. I never saw her again. After the DNA tests came back, saying the family was not ours, she called me a couple of times, certain that the test was wrong. She wanted me to come back. I'm not sure why I couldn't bring myself to go back. I considered it. Otherwise my family search had come to an end. There were no more leads, our records had simply been misrecorded, mixed up with Namhee and Namjung somewhere along the way. Would it be so bad to fill this void for this family? Become Jung Namjung, their niece and cousin? But I just couldn't. Maybe it was because my Korean was not so good then and it felt like a burden to try to communicate with them. But likely it was because I could not bring myself to be adopted for a second time.

✈ **SHANNON DOONA HEIT**

9

GOING BACK

In 1986, when I was eighteen years old, I travelled to South Korea with a group of adoptees—some with their adoptive parents—but I was one of those who travelled alone since my adoptive parents didn't share or even understand my wish to see the country where I was born. Deep down in my heart, I hoped to meet my father and my sisters.

Before leaving I got in touch with the Norwegian adoption agency; I'd written a letter with many questions, and they forwarded it to Holt Children's Services in Korea. One evening, towards the end of my two weeks there, I got a phone call. My Norwegian guide told me that someone from Holt had been walking door-to-door in the town where I was born, showing a picture of me at about a year and six months old to the residents. Finally—finally, someone had recognized me! I'm not sure whether he had met one of my sisters, or someone else who knew them but God bless him for doing that. I got the message that I would meet my Korean family in the early evening the next day. I was so shocked that my mind went blank and stayed that way for the rest of the day. I could not believe that I was going to meet family—my real family—after all those years of yearning to see from where I came.

At last I met with one uncle, two of my three sisters, their children, my oldest sister's husband, and a few cousins. I was overwhelmed. I'll never forget the moment when I gave my oldest sister a hug—the first one since I was a baby. My only thought was: I. Am. Home.

Despite not remembering my oldest sister's face anymore, I recognized her at a soul level. She described to me how, after our mother died, she used to carry me around when I was a baby. To finally feel that I belonged somewhere and that family truly cared about me became a very powerful moment for me. I was so used to adoptive parents who loved their alcohol bottles, who used to yell at me and beat me. The contrast was overwhelming. Here, at last, I was met with love and I cried with joy the whole time.

The same day, I got the bad news later on, which nearly devastated me. I had arrived ten years too late to see him—the one person whom I'd longed to meet during all the lost years. My Korean father—my *appa*—my treasure, was gone. When my *appa* handed me to the orphanage, he wasn't told that he would never see me again. Our father loved all of us children, but he needed help during a difficult time to make a better life for us. He died while he searched for me, still hoping to find me and bring me back home. He never knew how far away I really was—that I had been sent almost five thousand miles away to Norway, the land of the Vikings, and into the hands of a strangers. I felt as if someone had torn away a piece of my heart. This has affected my oldest Korean sister's life too. She yearned for me for so many years, and promised our *appa* on his death bed that she would continue his search, so that we could one day be together.

Today, it's been more than twenty-five years since my trip back to Korea. I have not been able to return. It hurts to think back to that time, and my heart continues to feel empty. I have to visit my motherland at least once more, while am I still young enough and have my health. My dream is to complete the circle by standing beside my real parents' grave. I never met them again, having longed for them all my life, I no longer have any memory of their faces, their voices have been silent for too long, and I don't know the way home.

About one hour's driving outside of Seoul a house still stands. There we lived, where I was born, where my parents made their living. I hope one day to take a glance at this part of my history. It's more than forty years since I was taken away. Korea is part of me, but I'm a stranger there, a tourist. I don't speak the language, and I don't know the customs or the culture in my motherland. Deep down in my heart I will love Korea forever, because that is where my parents are resting. A part of me will never forget. But I will never return to stay; that ship has sailed, a long, long time ago.

I keep in touch with my oldest sister by email; she doesn't understand English, but her son speaks some and translates as best as he can. I'm grateful to have had this experience, to have met my family, and my sister has even been here in Norway to visit, a few years ago. I realize that I will always be an outsider all those years separated is too great of a barrier. My childhood dream is gone forever: I know that I can no longer think or dream that, one day, I could just move back and jump in, catching up where I left off. We are family, but have become strangers to each other, and this makes me sad. My heart is torn in half, with one foot in Norway, and one in Korea, for the rest of my life.

✈

The sound of ocean waves lapping against the shore and childhood giggling, soft wind caressing our faces, the warm rays of the sun keep me and my good Norwegian friend Vanja warm on a beautiful summer's day. Along the beach, two little boats embellished by precious sea shells hand-picked by our small hands float on tiny waves. Now and then, little red and green crabs would hang on and enjoy a free ride. We laughed so hard as we pushed the boats out to meet their destiny while we shouted "Ship ahoy!". We spent hours catching the little crabs and tiny shrimps, the transparent ones that slipped away so easily, and sometimes we even caught small fish. We built sand castles, and decorated them with beautiful sea shells.

Korean Adoptees, Then and Now

I cherish this Norwegian memory so much because it is one of the few nice, warm ones that remain from my childhood. The beach, the boats, Vanja and me. This is among the first things that I can consciously recall. But why must I divide my childhood into before and after I was sent out of Korea? This is not the natural way of things.

My life, and my childhood, began in Korea. I had my family around me. I heard their voices, and I understood what they said. I smiled at my mum and dad as every baby does. Life was sounds, smells, caresses and love. I was one of four sisters, the youngest, and I was cared for by everyone. I cannot recall any of this as clearly as I do the Norwegian memory described above. My Korean memories are buried deep inside me and feel like a black hole sometimes. My first family was my everything, my whole world, comfort and safety, all that was dear to me. It's as if Korea has been erased.

Then came the adoptoraptors, in my case the Holt agency, who took me away from it all and threw me out into adoptionland. All that I knew, all that was important and safe, was suddenly lost. My family and heritage was wiped out with lies on paper. My Hojuk, my family registration paper, was falsified by a typewriter. On it, they wrote "Father: No record, Mother: No record," even though my father's name was mentioned on other papers. With just a few pen strokes, they sealed my destiny, turned me into an orphan with no one who cared for me, to make me much more suitable and attractive for a quick foreign adoption.

The agency, with the blessing of the state of Korea, robbed me of my family and sold me for profit to a foreign land is a criminal violation of my human rights. And once I had been bought and shipped to my new home, the state of Norway falsified my birth certificate and wrote my adoptive parents down as my biological ones. This is grotesque. I was never theirs, I did not come from them, I was never in my adoptive mother's womb. I was taken by Holt without the consent of my still living Korean father. He was never asked, nor told that I had been sent out of the country, and he spent many years searching for me in Korea. It was a criminal act committed against me and my family.

THE "UNKNOWN" CULTURE CLUB

And yet the act against us has been covered, turned into something that is supposed to be beautiful, and called Adoption. I wonder if the world will ever understand the unfathomable loss that adoption represents for adoptees and their natural families. Will it understand why justice means so much? It is more than just a word, it's about our worth as human beings.

In recent years, I have read newspaper articles in which Holt admitted to falsifying the Hojuks of the Korean children they obtained for adoption. It was simply too much work, too cumbersome, to check whether children were actually orphans, and whether they were truly eligible for adoption. It was much more efficient and convenient to simply fabricate a piece of paper saying that there were no parents and no family.

It is time for Holt to make an official apology to all Korean adoptees for their fraudulent practice and offer some kind of compensation for the pain we've had to endure. One fitting good-will gesture might be to offer free flight tickets to Korea, so that adoptees could visit their country of birth, and thus find help in healing wounds—permanent separations from family and the nation. We've earned it. Through the years we've contributed greatly to Korea's growth and Holt's profit, and the business is still going strong. *They owe us!*

And at the end of the day, why is Holt still allowed to continue their practice of what many of us informed adult adoptees call legalized kidnapping? How many more must be sent abroad to uncertain destinies? When will enough be enough? Have they not sent enough children out of Korea by now? And how much longer will the world watch with open eyes and accept that this madness still goes on?

✈ **KHARA NINE**

10

LETTER FROM GRANDMOTHER

Sometimes humans do things with a lot of hesitation and other times humans do not think much before taking action. In my case, I would at least contemplate before acting—especially if it was something I felt would be important. Strangely enough, when it came to the search for my biological family in Korea, I just did it with an open mind, not afraid of misery or rejection. Strange how life can change suddenly for the better or for the worse. The reason I started looking was mostly out of curiosity. I wondered: *Who are they and how do they live their lives?* The need to look for my Korean family and even meet with them for my own sake or knowing more of myself hadn't, previously, entered my mind. I was satisfied with my life.

At the same time I didn't know what I might find—if anything. *How could I?* I never had any pictures or stories about my Korean family. I had only the names of my Korean grandmother and mother documented on paper. And I hadn't made up any imaginary pictures of their appearance or their demeanor.

The only thing I knew about my Korean origin was that my biological mother had been in an accident as a child and that she was being cared for by my grandparents. My Korean "backpack" while growing up in Sweden was very light, which was most convenient, perhaps. It's really hard to say if this lack of data made me wait for so long to make a search. Maybe, if I had more information, I would have been satisfied, and not look. *Who knows?* After all is said and done, I still think I would have been curious to know more.

What really made me decide to look was due to one of my best friends also adopted from Korea. Having a close friend talk about the relationship he had with his biological family made the possibility of a reunion feel real. He also believed it was important for him to inspire me to try to find my people as well.

It seemed that events went really fast when the trip planning started rolling. I received an email message quickly with the news that the Social Welfare Society (SWS) had found my mother and grandma!

After emailing my information to this organization, I heard back after only waiting for one and a half months. The possibility of a reunion all of a suddenly felt real: *They were alive!* Today, the news may not seem so big, but back then—early in the summer of 2012—it was a very big deal for me!

Later that summer, I got the first letter from my Korean grandmother packaged together with some pictures of the family. My mother had an accident when she was only six years old. After that, her mental health, cognitive and spatial ability gradually deteriorated. At age twenty-one or twenty-two she gave birth to me. I was then already processed for adoption and flown to Sweden at only three months old. That's the youngest age I've heard babies sent overseas.

Of course, I felt sadness for my Korean mother's mental state and physical disability. Still, I prepared myself, believing that regardless of her disability, she is my mother. Furthermore, all my life in Sweden I have had a loving mother, so this experience didn't affect me too much. I was, and still am, just happy that I have met her.

My grandmother was touched and overwhelmed that I was looking for my mother. It was such a heart-wrenching feeling for her she couldn't find the words to explain. She also wrote she was happy and thankful for me looking them up. Reading that letter amplified my feelings, and I cried intensely. I was so happy. Now my family felt like a reality.

I sent back a letter and, in September of 2012, received a second reply from my grandmother translated by the adoption agency:

Dear my grandson,

I was happy to receive your letter. After hearing from you, I searched for Sweden on a globe wondering where it is. When I think of you who has been missing mom from far away, my heart aches a lot.

And it is generous of you to understand us and never to blame us. I do appreciate you for saying so. Having read your letter, I feel you are really considerate and good-hearted.

I wonder you might have been discriminated against a lot because of the color of your skin, which makes me more sorry and sad.

It is grateful that your adoptive parents have raised you well so far. I want you not to forget their favor and be good to your parents. Your birth mom fell down from on high up thirty years ago. After she got a brain surgery, though, her brain was getting worse so she has been suffering for around thirty years. Now her intellectual level is on two or three-year old baby.

You have seven cousins from three to fifteen-year old. At that time when we put you up for adoption, your aunt and uncles were too young to know about it so they have no idea that you exist. Please don't be too disappointed about that.

I understand you might be disappointed though you have missed and looked for your mom for so long. No matter how your mom is, I pray every day to Buddha that you are able to pursue your goal to the end and live your life confidently. Take care of yourself.

Love,
Your grandma

The emailing continued for almost one and a half years, and I was just happy with that.

In the fall of 2013, I was invited to visit my adopted friend who at the time lived in Korea. I spontaneously said, "yes!" I should take a chance and meet my grandma!

Just a few days before leaving for Korea, I got another translated letter from her saying that she agreed to meet me. The thought gave me an obvious thrill.

But I didn't dwell in advance, or imagine how our meeting would be. I can't say that the thought felt surreal, but I believed I was about to do something historical—considering how little my life had been about Korea thus far. I was about to enter unknown territory. Together, with a social worker, I finally met my grandmother and mother, at the adoption agency, January 2014, two days before my birthday.

The first time I saw my biological mother, she was lying on the floor napping, in a place where one is "not supposed to" be sleeping. On this particular occasion, she had one of those days when she lost her balance, fell and hit the floor. The reason for this fall was caused by her imbalance gait. She can walk, but has trouble and it can be determined by looking at her that something is wrong. Before our meeting, I was already prepared for this type of thing because of the letters written to me by my grandmother.

Just like my thought before, but unlike many other adoptee stories, the reunion didn't feel surreal. Rather, a warm and familiar sensation dominated, combined with a this is a very special moment intimacy. *Isn't it strange how a meeting like this can feel so familiar, like we already know each other?*

One of the first things my grandmother said was that she was sorry—so sorry for giving me away for adoption. She had already written this many times in previous letters, reminding me of how much guilt she must have felt during all those years. But apart from that, this historical meeting was just exciting and joyful. I immediately felt that warm sentiment of true love, and I'm sure my grandma felt the same. I also guessed quickly, that she must be an open, relaxed, uncomplicated and easy-going person. For that I am happy, because that also set the tone for our first meeting after twenty-nine years apart.

My grandma was happy to see that I had grown up to become an healthy, well-mannered, successful and reasonable adult. And my hope was that the photos I brought would fill the twenty-nine years spanning an ocean of time that had passed—at least to some degree.

The first meeting with my Korean family was a very positive outcome despite learning that my grandfather died in 1993. I was glad to hear that my grandma said that we should stay in contact—something I hadn't taken for granted beforehand. During that trip, I got to visit her home several times, and I stayed in touch with her when I returned to Sweden in March.

I quickly traveled back to Korea in August of the same year. It was my desire to see my grandmother and be in my motherland again, a place I still love to be. The ambience just drew me back. Despite the language barrier, it felt so natural to be with my grandmother. I feel a great connection. I never felt "unsure of my identity" or anything growing up, but I felt an immediate bond with my Korean grandmother. She is my family. She doesn't 'replace' my Swedish family, nor my Swedish adoptive grandmother. She is my grandmother in Korea, an important role, too, at least for me. She is a link to not only my biological roots—I also have two aunts and uncles and several cousins—but also the Korean culture I never got to experience. (just saying it, I'm not bitter.) Since she is such a warm-hearted person, I really want to be with her and stay in touch. My Korean grandmother was also the first biological family member I met, therefore she will always have a special place in my heart.

Without comparing, since that would be difficult and pointless, I can easily say that I now have two families. They don't exclude each other. For me, that's not strange. It's just a great favor that life has given me. But it comes with a variety of feelings. Again, without comparing or ranking my Swedish and Korea families, it should be said that thinking of my grandmother not only makes me happy but also emotional, because she embodies my Korean origin. I don't know if I will be able to continue to visit her every year in the future, but the desire to stay in touch will not disappear. She takes care of my mother, therefore I have been thinking of what would happen when my grandmother passes away. She has told me that she is planning to send my mother to an institution then. I am a bit worried about how that would be for her. As long as my grandma has the health and energy, my mom can't have a better place to be.

If at all possible, I'm pretty sure I would visit her. Even if she can't talk, she is still my mother. I'm not sure whether she knows who I am or not but I can see that we are similar in appearance, a comfort I never had while growing up in Sweden.

My time spent in Korea, mainly meetings with my grandmother, has not replaced my Swedish identity, but has actually added a small part of a Korean identity, and a desire to take in so much more knowledge about and experiences from my birth country. It was not difficult to add that layer on top of my solid Swedish identity - probably just because my upbringing was so grounded. On some occasions though, the *melting together* of the two identities has stirred more feelings inside. Emotional, yes. Confusing, not really - it hasn't changed the foundation of who I am. But it surely has started some sort of process. I think it would be strange if such a thing didn't make any friction at all.

Speaking of melting identities together, this summer I will take my Swedish parents to Korea, and visit my grandmother with them. Again, it's impossible to know how it will feel, making both "worlds" come together. But I'm pretty certain it will go well. I will go back to Korea many times, but since it might be the only time my Swedish parents will go, meeting my grandma will for sure be a unique experience for them.

What the exploration with my Korean family will mean to me in the long run remains to be seen. For now, I'm just happy with the connection I have made. My grandmother has also confided that she will introduce me to the rest of the family on my mother's side (since my father is unknown). At this point, only my aunt who lives in Seoul knows about my existence and one of my uncles learned by accident. He arrived a day earlier while I was staying at my grandma's house last summer but our surprise meeting went well. To the rest of the family, I have been kept a secret

THE "UNKNOWN" CULTURE CLUB

during all those years. I have a whole family who I hope to meet in the future. I am happy that my grandmother wants to tell them about me but even if that never happens, I will always be in touch with her.

✈ROBIN HÖGBERG

11

REMEMBER ME

While growing up, my adoption was merely a series of facts about the first few months of my life. It was the prologue to my "actual" life the one that started when the plane landed in the United States. While the facts remain unchanged, the way I understand and make meaning of those facts has evolved a great deal, and that is the basis of the narrative that I share now. In other words, the story I am telling today is not the one I would have told five years ago, nor will it likely be the one I tell five years from now. Inevitably, with new experiences come new chapters, but even more importantly are the revisions of the way I understand my past. Allow me to explain.

I was born in Seoul, South Korea and adopted at three-months old, right around the peak of Korean adoptions in 1985, because my Korean mother was young and single. *Even though she loved me very much, she put me up for adoption because she thought it was for my best interest.* That was the story my loving adoptive parents shared, the story I could recite to others without thinking, the story that I knew without question. For the next twenty-five years, that introduction would remain in the background, relatively unexamined.

Being a Korean adoptee did not become a salient part of who I am until quite recently when I decided to quit my job and return to school for something I am passionate about, psychology. I have always been interested in race and culture, perhaps because my experiences seemed out of line with those around me. When I was about eight years old, I remember my father, with the best intentions, telling me to "take off my White mask." It was strange to consider at the time, given that for so long I had desperately wanted to change my *Asian* face. If I had a White mask, then why would I spend so much time playing with my eyes in the mirror to make them appear bigger? Why would I fall asleep every night pinching my nose hoping that it would somehow grow narrower? Looking back, I know my father was trying to be supportive and saying that I should not be ashamed of my Asian and Korean heritage, however, *back then, I would have given anything to have a White mask.*

Just like most children and adolescents, my goal was to "fit in" as much as possible. However, to me, "fitting in" entailed more than having friends or being a part of the cool crowd. As a Korean ADoptee (KAD), fitting in with the predominantly White European American community that I grew up in also meant aspiring to be White. Of course becoming White was not possible, but with the power of denial, I had managed to convince myself that *racism does not apply to me because I don't have it that bad.* My desire to blend in was so strong that I reasoned because I was not overtly bullied and because I felt White, I basically was White. At the time, being oblivious to racism served me well because I was able to function and be relatively happy. However, unbeknownst to me, I had internalized a great deal of racism in the form of yearning to be White and embarrassment about being Asian American and Korean. As a child, it is difficult to not be ashamed of something when it is not reflected anywhere. It is even more complicated to try to embrace something one does not understand and is rarely, if ever, exposed to.

Although I never appreciated being told by strangers that I was "lucky" to be adopted, I do love my adoptive family with all my heart. For a very long time, they were the only family that mattered. I did not understand why people would ask if I ever wanted to meet my "real" family. My automatic retort was, 'No need to, thanks. I already know my *real* family." My distaste for the question was not because I felt anger toward my Korean family—I just felt nothing at all. *How could strangers across the world whom I've never met be any more real than the family I was brought up in?*

Unfortunately, I lost my adoptive mother to cancer when I was ten years old. People like to say children are resilient. While I agree to an extent, for me, "resilience" was less about being strong and moving on. It was more about not fully understanding loss or how to deal with it. Although at the time I appeared relatively unscathed, looking back as an adult, I can see how losing two mothers at such a young age ingrained a profound sense of loss. Not that I was a noticeably sad person growing up, but that feeling of uncertainty and unsettledness became part of who I was. When my father remarried, I remember worrying, *Oh no, my stepmother better watch out because I cannot seem to keep a mother.* Luckily, my stepmom and stepsisters are still a major part of my life and my family.

I used to consider the death of my adoptive mother as a *real* loss, whereas I thought of my birth mother as more of a symbolic loss. I now realize that they were both very real in their own ways. One reason I never had a visceral yearning to meet my family of birth was because, for a long time, I did not think it was possible to lose something I never really knew. On the other hand, the thought of initiating a search was just too scary. I had already lost my adoptive mother and I did not want to lose my birth mother yet again. I feared that I would not be able to find my birth mother or, even worse, she would not want to be found. In my mind, by starting a search process I would be opening the door to a possible dead end, but if I never opened that door the possibility would always exist. Of course, I can see the inherent contradiction: I was attempting to protect myself from the pain of not finding my birth family by not even looking. The truth is that I was rather ambivalent probably because my Korean family meant so much to me. I did not consciously think about my Korean mother until the first class I took about adoption in graduate school. We were reading a chapter about birth parents and I remember feeling genuinely surprised and a little guilty when I realized that I had never thought about her on my birthday. My birthday! The one day we shared, and in 25 years she had never crossed my mind. Although trivial, this realization is when she went from being an abstract idea to a real person in my mind. I started to wonder, *does my Korean birth mom ever think about me? Does she remember me?*

I would have never predicted that my decision to switch careers, from business to psychology, would be so intricately linked to my KAD identity exploration. Academia gave me a space to start exploring race, national origin, and adoption, which became an opportunity to begin a personal journey that has been both difficult and rewarding. Perhaps I was drawn to psychology because there was a part of me that sought to understand my own experiences and context. Specifically, pursuing a career in clinical psychology might have been driven by the part of me that connects with people who are in pain. A serendipitous consequence of researching adoption has been discovering the vast and vibrant Korean adoptee community. Connecting with other adoptees has been invigorating. Here, I feel like I can share stories within a community without having to explain myself. It was other adoptees who encouraged me to go to the 2013 International Korean Adoptee Association's Gathering in Seoul. I figured it would be a good opportunity to present my research and explore the city I was born in so I decided to go.

For months before the trip, people asked if I was excited; I found it difficult to respond because, honestly, I wasn't quite sure how I felt. All I knew was that I wanted to explore Korea and meet other adoptees. Although I wanted to avoid the pressure and anxiety of a birth family search on my first trip, I decided that I would go to the agency to see if they had any information that I might find useful if I ever decided to search in the future. Before the trip, my father dug up all of the adoption records he had, which consisted of a few medical files, adoption papers, and travel documents. I had never known my birth weight and height so merely sifting though those records and learning random facts about my first days, like that I drank barley tea in between milk feedings, was an intensely validating experience. Even though the information was rather trivial, looking at these records made me feel like a real person who lived in Korea. There was finally proof of the first three months of my existence, which made the facts feel more like lived experience, even though I had no actual memory of my life in Korea. I felt satisfied being equipped with this new information. I thought if I found nothing at the adoption agency in Korea, at least this was worthwhile.

As the plane approached Incheon Airport, I gazed out of my window and the beauty of the mountainous landscape blew me away. I was not expecting mountains! When I arrived in Seoul, I thought about how the city I was born in felt so foreign to me now. As I strolled down the street by myself and felt the stares of local Koreans, I wondered if they could tell that even though I was from there, that I was not *from* there. I felt much more at ease once the conference began and I was surrounded by hundreds of KADs from across the world. Despite our different cultures and languages, we were there and united by our early pasts. Looking around the room, I realized the countless possible lives I could have lived: I could have grown up on the west coast of the United States; I could have been French or Danish. I could have been sent almost anywhere! I was struck by the arbitrariness of adoption, while at the same time, I felt thankful that the randomness inherent in the beginning of our lives brought us all together in that moment and for that week.

My roommate connected me with the four adoption agencies that had set up booths for the conference and I made an appointment to visit Holt and look at my file midweek. A few nights before the big day I was eating dinner with some other adoptees who advised me to be prepared for a very emotional experience and even suggested that I bring someone with me. Typically, I am cautious with my emotions and I usually do take the time to "prepare" myself as much as possible, but I did not see a need to do so for this. I reasoned that I was probably not going to find much more information than I had before I left; I was just doing my due diligence while in Korea. Taking the advice of the other adoptees, I invited someone who I had met at the conference a few days prior to accompany me at the agency.

Korean Adoptees, Then and Now

The Korean social worker greeted us warmly. She seated us in the conference room while she fetched my file. When she returned, she placed the file on the table and calmly and casually said, "So your birth mother stopped by the agency five years ago. She left you this letter."

I thought I had misheard the social worker and was confused when she actually pulled out pages of bright yellow notepaper with Korean handwriting. Some stationary is decorated with little pictures or pleasant words or expressions. Ironically, this paper had a quote in English on the top that said, "Remember Me." I wondered if it was a coincidence or if my Korean mother knew what it meant.

I only made it through the first paragraph before I started crying with tears of joy, guilt, longing, and a strange sense of empathy. I was grateful to have someone with me to share one of the most pivotal days of my life. Had he not been there, I am not sure I would have remembered much. The letter hit me hard and unexpectedly. My time at the agency felt like a confusing blur, with my mind cloudy, eyes puffy, and heart heavy. The letter, which had already been translated, had been patiently waiting for me in my file for five years. I would reread the letter dozens of times that night so that it was practically memorized. I felt moved by holding a physical artifact from my Korean mother and a sense of connection from simply touching the paper she had touched. I was stunned by this unexpected twist in my story. That day, I learned more about my past than I had in my entire life. I learned what my Korean mother was doing, that I had a brother, and most importantly in my mind, that she wanted to meet me. For such a long time I had prepared myself for the possibility that she did not want to meet me. I was so focused on the negative *what if's* that I had never even fathomed a letter saying the opposite. The letter answered my questions that spawned my interest in adoption research: *does my Korean mother ever think about me? Does she remember me? Yes.* The answer was yes and I was overwhelmed with relief and joy.

I asked the adoption agency to let her know that I read the letter, was very excited, and would write back soon. After a couple weeks of unsuccessful attempts to contact her, the social worker had to get Korean Adoption Services (KAS) involved. During the next month, back in the United States, I got lost yet again in all of the *what-ifs*. *What if she died? What if she changed her mind?* One morning, I woke up to news from Korea: my birth mother was shocked and excited to hear I had read her letter and she wanted to be in touch with me. The email with this wonderful news included her name, address, phone number, and email address. All of a sudden I knew her name! Initially, contact felt like it was just a click away. The complications of language and cultural barriers were far in the back of my mind. I felt like all of my senses were temporarily heightened. On the drive to school I noticed that the world was the same, but that I was seeing everything differently. I was appreciating things that I never paid attention to before: the junctures on trees where the branches come together, the shapes of shadows and silhouettes of landscapes. I thought about how, many times, appreciation involves loss. That morning, I felt lucky that I was appreciating the world because I had gained something. I thought about my Korean mother, on the other side of the world, wondering how she was feeling with this news.

Since that morning we have exchanged pictures and written a few emails back and forth. With each letter I learn a little bit more about her and, therefore, a little more about myself. The euphoria has waxed and waned. There are times when I feel so frustrated we are separated by language and culture. I find myself wishing things were easier. In one of her letters she said, "our emotions and cultures are different. There will be awkward and uncomfortable moments." Yes. Yes, they are and, yes, there will be. I am thankful that she pointed that out. My Korean mother is a strong and thoughtful woman. Her story, inherently connected with my own, is one that is filled with ups and downs. Nevertheless, it is her story, and I will leave it for her to share one day because she plans to write about her own life.

We sometimes tell ourselves stories to help us make sense of the world. What we do not do enough is pay attention to how the stories we tell change and how these changes reflect meaning far above and beyond their actual content. My story has undergone substantial shifts between the background and foreground. It started with adoption being a small detail about something that

Korean Adoptees, Then and Now

happened to me. Now, I am not just adopted; *I am an adoptee*. It defines me. It helps me answer that perplexing question, *who am I?* I've also learned the important lesson that the way we tell these stories has real implications on what we do, the things we seek out, and our openness to the experiences that find us. Not going to the adoption agency would have been one of the biggest mistakes of my life, but I would not have even known it.

Just like any story, mine will continue to develop in unexpected ways. Lately, I find myself pondering and revising my notion of *home* and *where I am from*. I guess, for now, *from* is less about geography and more about family. While I was born in Korea and I grew up in the United States, I am from both my Korean and American families. My birth mother signs her letters, *your Korean mother*. As I get to know her, I wonder if the qualification *birth* in *birthmother* will become less salient and what it will mean to know her simply as *my Korean mother* or just plain *mother*. She also calls me Ae Kyung, a person who ceased to exist in my mind when I arrived in the United States and became Danielle. Now, with our reunion and my recent immersion into the KAD community, my Korean identity has been resurrected, although—according to my Korean mother—*Ae Kyung*, the baby she birthed, has never stopped existing. I am excited to see how these meanings evolve and to be able to look back at this written piece, which reflects but a snapshot in time.

✈ **DANIELLE GODON-DECOTEAU**
AE KYUNG KIM

12

SOME SCARS ARE WORN ON THE INSIDE

Some scars are worn on the inside. They are safely hidden away from the outside world, invisible to others, even the ones closest to you. My name is Simone and I'm a Korean adoptee. My given Korean name is Kuihee.

I was born in South Korea in 1971 to a family who already had four children. I was the fifth and the youngest. My biological parents struggled financially and divorced when I was one year old. Subsequently each parent remarried and both had more children with their new spouses. My older siblings and I were shuffled back and forth between the new families, until ultimately my father decided to place me for adoption.

At almost five years old, I boarded a plane headed for Switzerland. I was quarantined for a few days before at last meeting my adoptive family on September 18, 1976. I have lots of memories from that day, and this is really when my memories started in earnest. Prior to that day I have only very vague memories. For example, I don't remember my biological siblings, my Korean mother nor my Korean father, nor my time at the orphanage. I believe that being abandoned at the orphanage was so traumatic, that my mind blocked it out. My adoptive mom told me that

Korean Adoptees, Then and Now

during my quarantine I was so upset and combative, that the people there gave me valium syrup to calm me down. Why would anyone be surprised by my outbursts? Imagine that you lose your entire family, then live with strangers and a horde of other children who come and go as they were being processed, flown to a foreign country where you suddenly don't understand anyone and everybody looks different from you. Anyway, they handed the bottle to my adoptive mom urging her to give me some if I were to become too agitated. Needless to say my adoptive mom never gave me any of the valium—there was no need. I adjusted surprisingly quickly.

During the first few months I would stash my belongings in my bed. When my adoptive parents bought me my first pair of shoes, I was so excited and when it was time to go to sleep I took them to bed with me. My adoptive mom said that I awoke that night yelling bloody murder. My shoes had disappeared! Well, they hadn't disappeared, of course. My adoptive mom had just removed them when I was sleeping. I got up to discover that they were gone. I was so upset. It took a while for me to realize that what was mine was still mine even if it wasn't in my immediate sight and touch at all times. My adoptive family gave me the structure of a family, love, and a sense of belonging that every child needs and craves. I feel a very strong and close bond with them.

Still, even with all that love, I felt out of place, alone, and often isolated growing up in a country where everyone was white, had big round eyes and large noses. I had many encounters with racism which left me angry and deeply hurt. It was a difficult time which was compounded by the fact that being "Swiss" was all I knew and although I felt Swiss on the inside and I tried very hard to fit in, there was this nagging sense of never truly belonging.

I first searched for my Korean family when I was nineteen years old. However, at that time communication between a Switzerland-founded organization called Terre des Hommes and Korea Social Services had stopped and I was advised to travel to South Korea and contact the police directly. At nineteen, traveling overseas wasn't something I wanted to do or was ready for. I also believed that mothers who remarried would often deny the existence of their previous children because their new spouses weren't aware of their previous relationships or children, and that puts the mothers in a difficult situation when being contacted years later by their much older adopted-out children. I assumed that this was the case with my mother, so I shelved the idea of searching for her for over twenty years. I got married, moved to the United States and had children of my own.

Then one night, in the autumn of 2013, I dreamt that I met a woman and we hugged each other. I couldn't make out her face but I instinctively knew that this woman was my Korean mother. I woke feeling really peculiar. Normally, I can barely remember any of my dreams. However, this dream felt like a premonition and I had to give it one last try! My birth parents were getting older and time was starting to run out if I was to find them.

It's difficult to explain how now and then things just fall into place without much effort. While my search was underway, I was accepted for a homeland tour back to Korea with Me & Korea (Mosaic Tour) for the summer of 2014. This would be my first time traveling to the country of my birth. I was asked by the tour guide if I was interested in searching for my family and I explained that I had already started one. However, because I hadn't heard back from Korea Social Services and knew the process could take anywhere from six to twelve months, I allowed for the Mosaic Tour to conduct an independent search.

And then came the phone call that turned my world upside down. Mosaic Tour told me that two of my brothers were located in Korea—a mere nine days after they started looking into my information. I couldn't believe what I was hearing: They. Were. Found. I was flooded with so many emotions. A lot of joy but also deep sadness. I tried to process that there were two men in Korea, and they were my biological brothers. I learned that my Korean father had passed away some time ago and that they were still looking for my mother. I wondered what my brothers looked like, what they were like, and where my mother was. My dream would become reality after all.

Strangely, no contact was made with my brothers prior to me going to Korea. I would have preferred an initial written contact at first, but I learned that Sergeant Lee, was a Korean police officer, who had found my brothers, usually conducted reunions in this manner. That meant that I had plenty of time to daydream about my siblings and not a day went by that I didn't think of them. I was imagining our first meeting. In preparing for the reunion, I talked to other adoptees who had already met with their families. The most important advice I received was to not expect too much, and go into it with an open mind. I think that was really sound advice. As my trip approached, I started to hear about unhappy reunions, or some that never came to fruition because the birth family refused to meet. It suddenly dawned on me that there is really no guarantee for a happy outcome. What if my brothers didn't want to meet me? Perhaps they didn't know of my existence, then what? Now I was really nervous! I thought to myself, "What did I get myself into?"

Preparing for my trip I was transported back to my childhood days when I would go to overnight camps. There was this nervous excitement going through the packing list, checking it, and making sure I had absolutely thought of everything and packed everything. I bought gifts for my host family stay, school children, and for my brothers. And while I packed the gifts, I prayed that I would not have to bring these items back with me, while at the same time preparing myself mentally should a meeting fail.

I have travelled a lot in my life. I have flown many times, but no flight was as significant as the one to Seoul. After thirty-eight years I would touch down on Korean soil again, see Korea and its people again, and eat authentic Korean food again. I felt lucky beyond words. I also felt there was a lot riding on this. Would I be let down or would this be the trip of a lifetime? There was no way of knowing. It was truly a leap of faith.

My first attempt of making contact with one of my brothers was on the first full day of the tour. We had just toured Gyeongbokgung Palace and finished eating our lunch in Insadong when I was told that I was going to go to my brother's house, about an hour's drive from Seoul. Okay. this is the moment I was waiting for so long and it was finally here. I felt shaky. I was so overcome with emotions that I just balled. I'm not much of a crier but right there and then the tears just flowed, uncontrollably and unstoppable. We were en route to his place when new information came

THE "UNKNOWN" CULTURE CLUB

trickling in. It turned out that a police officer previously tried to contact my brother a couple of times and it seemed that nobody answered. This could mean that he was either out of town, or that he had a business which required him to be out most of the day. Would I still want to go forward with a potential reunion even though he most likely wouldn't be there? I didn't think this made much sense, so I decided to return to my tour group. To most people this would not be very devastating. *So he wasn't there, just try another time.* However, this moment was months in the making for me. For months I had been waiting for this, and now, I turned around. I was extremely upset and just cried and cried.

The tour was almost over when we attempted to visit my brother's place a second time. This time Sgt. Lee accompanied me personally along with the director of Mosaic Tours. No one was home at my brother's place, so we ate dinner at a nearby restaurant before returning to the apartment buildings where my brother lived. We sat there all night long, with Sgt. Lee periodically checking to see if my brother had returned. No one returned or answered the door, so Sgt. Lee left a message at the door. Speaking with neighbors he learned that my brother had small children and was sometimes absent from his apartment for a longer amount of time. Again, I returned to the group without a successful meeting. Honestly, by then I thought to myself: Who isn't home for months on end? He must be avoiding me. I was genuinely discouraged. It was possible that this meeting just wasn't in the cards for me.

It was Friday night and time for the tour's farewell concert. The concert was beautiful and very emotional, I cried several times because it was so touching. I was behind the curtain with my fellow tour members, about to go onstage to sing when the tour's director came running, "Simone! Simone, your brother is on his way to see you!" I was absolutely stunned. I couldn't believe that after all the times we tried unsuccessfully, it would be that easy

. I felt utterly unprepared. Holy crap, this is going to happen tonight. This is absolutely crazy. I somehow managed to go onstage and sing with my group. After the concert had finished I impatiently waited for my brother to arrive, which seemed to take an eternity. People shouldn't have to wait thirty-eight years, nine days, and a couple of hours to see their brother.

When I saw my brother come up the steps, my heart sure skipped a beat. It was a very surreal moment. We hadn't seen each other since I was four and he was seven years old. And now, there we stood, staring at each other. Every since I can remember I've had this hole inside me, that empty space that was just always there. Sometimes unnoticed, and not always felt, but always present. And from time to time it would rear its ugly head. When I hugged my brother, I could feel how that space was being filled. There was this wonderful sense of resolution that washed over me. My brother received a notice that I was looking for him that evening. He owns a restaurant and as soon as he knew I was in Korea, he literally dropped everything, sent his patrons home and closed the restaurant. Then he drove with his wife and son through heavy Friday night traffic from Incheon to Seoul.

I had so much to absorb and process. My brother was able to fill me in about my first few years in Korea and about my other siblings. I learned I have an older sister in Japan (there was no mention of a sister in my adoption file), my oldest brother lives in the United States and my youngest brother does a lot of traveling and isn't always in Korea. That explained his long absence from his home. I already knew that my Korean father had passed away many years earlier but not the exact circumstances of his passing. Sadly, my mother whom I thought I was still going to meet, had passed away only two years prior to my coming back to Korea. I feel this was a missed opportunity. I learned that my mother never consented to giving me up for adoption, and that she was distraught and heartbroken when she found out that I had already left the country. She and my younger brother kept looking for me all those years. It saddens me to know that my Korean mother died without ever seeing me again or learning what happened to her youngest daughter.

Amazingly, my youngest brother returned to Korea with his oldest son just a couple of days before my return flight. When I saw him for the first time I was floored at how much we looked alike. Pretty amazing to know you look like someone else and to know that you are blood-related. As an adoptee I have grown up without that visual affirmation, so seeing myself reflected in my brothers was extraordinary. My brother was clearly excited to have me back and because he spoke English there was no language barrier. We were able to communicate easily! We discovered our oldest sons are almost the exact same age and that he had stayed in Germany for a while, which is next to Switzerland!

What's interesting to me is that I have two younger half sister and half brother on my father's side who were also adopted. All this time I thought I was the only one who was adopted and now it turned out that the three of us were relinquished at the orphanage together. I have no recollection of that but perhaps being together with my siblings gave me a little bit of comfort. I am currently in the process of establishing contact with them. It's strange to know that I have so many siblings and that we are spread all over the world.

I'm so happy I was able to visit my Korean father's grave. It was situated on a tranquil, beautiful but very steep hill. My brother and I made the trek over the hills and I still remember how peaceful the place was. I cried softly as I said my good-byes to my father. Right there was the closest I would ever be with him. Admittedly, for many years I had feelings of resentment towards him for taking me to the orphanage, although deep inside I knew that he must have seen no other way for his family to stay afloat. It hurt to know that he was gone forever and I would never have the chance to talk to him. All this weighed heavily on me as tears streamed down my face. I desperately wanted to tell him that I loved him nonetheless and that I was grateful that he left accurate information at the orphanage which made it possible for me to find my family again. This was his last gift to me.

✈ **SIMONE RENDON LUTZ**

THIS IS MY BIRTH FATHER

Like many Korean adoptees,
I focus my disconnect to Korea to my birth mother,
Rather than my birth father,
In my falsified adoption documents.

I was told:
They weren't married,
I was illegitimate,
He abandoned my birth mother,
And I was sent to a baby home and then a foster home.

This isn't a rare occurrence,
But a template that agencies use,
To fill in the dates and other facts,
To make "orphan" Korean babies look desirable.

When I received information about my birth family,
My whole world shook in an instant.
My Korean parents were married—
Even before I was born, they were married.

THE "UNKNOWN" CULTURE CLUB

I had two older sisters,
My family was a rural poor working class family,
And they were convinced I'd be better off.
I guess those details weren't important enough to mention.

Since meeting my birth family face-to-face,
I see the loss and love they have for me.

I see a hardened Korean man soften when I smile at him.
This is my Korean birth father,
Who I thought didn't want me most of all.

But when we talk,
In my misspelled and broken Korean,
He listens and sees me.

With the help of technology,
I can have entire conversations on my phone.
To talk about anything with him.
I have yet to share my whole and true self with him—

But I will.
As we get to know one another,
As I continue to see myself in him,
I will.

✈ CHRISTINA SEONG

PART THREE:

"UNKNOWN" CLUB

15

BECOMING REAL

"Real isn't how you are made," said the Skin Horse. "It's a thing that happens to you. When a child really loves you for a long, long time, not just to play with, but really loves you, then you become Real."

"Does it hurt?" asked the Rabbit.

"Sometimes," said the Skin Horse, for he was always truthful.

"When you are Real you don't mind being hurt ... It doesn't happen all at once ... You become. It takes a long time ... Generally, by the time you are Real, most of your hair has been loved off, and your eyes drop out and you get loose in the joints and very shabby. But these things don't matter at all, because once you are Real you can't be ugly, except to people who don't understand."

From *The Velveteen Rabbit* by Margery Williams

You know the Velveteen Rabbit? Who wanted to become real? I feel like I became real when my daughter was born. Except, unlike the Rabbit, I didn't know that I was a toy before that. I thought I knew what love was, or what being human was, or who I was. But I didn't know any of that. Not really.

I didn't plan to get pregnant. That was a surprise to me. But I was engaged to her father at the time and I was over the age of thirty so I knew I wanted to keep her. To be fair, I considered abortion and adoption so I wouldn't have any regrets, but in my heart I always knew she was mine. I often say that I should go on tour to talk about sex education to high school students because I have personally lived a very important message. I would tell them: "It only takes one time being unprotected. One time, kids." Before, I was always very careful about that. Always. Like double-bag it careful. But he talked me into it. Looking back, I wonder if he did it on purpose. The day I found out I was pregnant was the same day I was going to break up with him. But I took a pregnancy test and when he walked in the door, instead of telling him it was over, I told him I was having a baby. He was happy. I thought my life was over and went downstairs to cry in my car alone.

People didn't know what a creep he was because many people think he was, and still is a sociopath. I didn't know what that was until recently. I thought sociopaths killed a lot of people. But some of them just walk around quietly destroying other people's lives. They're very charming on the outside but very tricky inside. I think I can't see them for who they are because there's a part of me that's empty inside and has no idea what real love is. Never knowing my own biological family, I wanted my daughter to have her biological father. At any cost. It didn't matter. My happiness, my sanity didn't matter. I begged him to be a good father and stay in her life even as he was abusing me.

I guess I went crazy for a while. Or maybe I'd always been crazy. And then, after I'd been broken down completely, I remembered who I was. Or maybe became something that I'd never been before. Well, anyway, I left him. It was the scariest thing I've ever done in my life. The one thing I never wanted to be was a single mom. I thought I would die, or somehow, cease to exist.

But I guess you could say that now, since I've done the scariest thing I could ever think of, I could probably pretty much do anything. Like jump out of a plane or climb a mountain. Except now I don't want to. Because I'm a mom and my life doesn't belong to me anymore: My life is about protecting myself so I can be around to raise my girl.

I don't have family. I grew up unloved. I was cared for in all the physical aspects. I had a roof over my head and food on a plate and I went to school (even when I was sick). But no one gave a shit about what I did or who I was as long as I got good grades and didn't embarrass anyone. After a year of being a mother myself, it really sunk in. I realized that I'd never known love until this little bundle of flesh plopped into my life. I love her with my whole heart. And I'd never been given that or received that. I was sure of it.

One day, after my daughter was a year old, I told my adoptive "mom" that I needed her to have a real relationship with me or it was over between us. She told me she was "too old" for that and we haven't spoken since. Not a single day goes by that I regret that. "Too old" was her code for "don't care." I knew in my heart that she didn't. It was kind of a relief to hear it firsthand, rather than pretending because the hurt finally stopped. Wishing for and wanting something that just didn't exist went away.

I raise my daughter alone without anyone's help. Her father, unable to control and manipulate me any longer, disappeared. And my adoptive "parents" never contacted me again. They even threw away everything they had of mine from my childhood, in case I was wondering if they held out any affinity for me whatsoever.

So, I am my mother. And by mother, I mean my Korean mother. She's my mother—even though I have no idea who she is—she just is. I guess whether she wants to be or not.

When I was a little girl growing up in Wisconsin, trapped in a household that told me I was going to hell for every sin I committed (and apparently I committed quite a few before the age of ten), where I would have been a Korean prostitute if they hadn't saved me, where the only thing I knew about Korea was that they buried stinking pots of rotting cabbage underground and ate it, I would dream, in short pieces, while lying in my bed alone at night before sleeping, about being with my mother. Living with her in a tiny apartment, in poverty. Like a tiny room with laundry hanging from a string. And, even if she had to work all the time and I only saw her one hour a week and just had rice to eat, I'd be happy.

I forgot about that dream. I had forgotten about it completely ... until I became my mother.

My daughter has no idea how good she has it. She has me every day, many hours a day, by my choice and, I guess, because we live in the U.S. We aren't as poor as my mother and I were in my dream. And even though society hates us (because what is worse than an unmarried single mother?), we have friends who don't hate us.

There are single mothers in Korea right now who are raising children on their own. I've heard that their families have abandoned them (for the shame) and they are keeping their children no matter the cost to them. I don't know a single one of them. But they are my kin.

People, especially adoptees, who think that their birth/natural mothers are horrible monsters for giving them up—well, I used to think that too—have no idea how f**king hard it is. I kept my daughter for love, yes, but I had a choice. When you live in a world where you're not given that choice, to overcome that is parallel to being a superhero. Sure, you can do it, but you have to commit feats of super-humanity and give up everything else you've ever known. I bet most of them didn't want to give away their children! But since they're forced to hide, we probably won't ever know. If it makes you feel any better, they're probably slowly dying inside anyway. Your absence is making them rot away starting with their heart.

I grew up with the impression that my mother and my father just didn't care. No one told me explicitly that they didn't care, but it was certainly implied, mainly by silence or by the putting down of Koreans that happened about once a year in my household. "Goddamn heathens" they were called. Anyway, being someone who grew a tiny person inside me and gave birth to that person and fell in love with her the instant I laid eyes on her, I bet most of them are in pain for the child they lost. These women are the shame of their nation but I think the persecutors should be ashamed of what they force families to do.

THE "UNKNOWN" CULTURE CLUB

I'm not really proud of being Korean. And I'm not particularly proud of being adopted. Or even American. I'm proud of being myself and raising my daughter and being an okay mom at least most of the time. Anyway, I try. Most people have no idea how hard it is. And that's all right. I know my daughter may never fully appreciate me and what I do either. And, honestly, that's really okay with me too. That's what love is.

✈ **PATTY SANG**

14

BURIED ROOTS

"You can't know where you're going if you don't know where you've been."

I've seen that quote pop up a hundred times—even by my (adoptive) family members. While I can appreciate what it means to most people, it's exceptionally frustrating for me as an adoptee denied of knowing my own roots. The double rub is knowing that my own family can't see how this affects me, because to most of them, my roots are theirs. When I was adopted, I supposedly inherited their family tree.

I don't fault my family for their way of thinking. I can't blame them for wanting to imagine me wholly theirs, because in my heart, I know their perspective originates from love. However, even in my forgiveness—my deep empathy for their perspective—I am hurt by it. I am more than what they see. I am more than what they want me to be. And I'm more than even what I, in all my self-awareness, know myself to be.

While growing up in the states, I was told I was found on the day I was born at the doorstep of a police station in Seoul, South Korea. "It meant you were loved," I was told, "because they knew you'd be safe." I wanted to believe that story so badly, but even as a kid, it didn't sit right with me.

I was also told, "The mothers who love their babies the most are the ones who give them up." I wanted to believe that, too. Yet before me, my parents had and kept two. And after that, they had and kept four more. Were my adoptive brothers and sisters less loved than me? It didn't appear so.

When I returned to South Korea and visited the adoption agency, I was told point blank that the story I knew was a lie. She didn't use that word, but she read me a different story about a baby being found on hospital grounds in Daegu—approximately one hundred and fifty miles from Seoul. My first estimated day of birth was written as March fifth—eleven days sooner than what became on record, with no explanation for the change. Confused by the vastly different story, I told her she must have had the wrong file. However, she read back my (adoptive) parents' names and address, supposedly confirming my beginnings.

After this, I wove in and out of accepting my new story. At times I was shocked and angry with my Korean mother—this phantom woman. After all, what kind of mother would leave a two week old infant outside in the cold of March? Other times I made excuses for her, imagining she knew I'd quickly be found. And as I learned more about the ghastly treatment of unwed mothers in Korea, I felt sorry for her. I pitied her trust that someone else could raise the baby she carried for nine months inside her, better than she. I labeled her as weak and misguided. I became livid at the thought of a relative stealing me away from her out of tough love. I went through every scenario and emotion because I knew I had absolutely nothing to go on.

Many adoptees build the courage and save the money to appear on Korean television shows. They air their first known photographs and the stories they've uncovered, hoping for someone to recognize them. At best, they'll uncover family whose been pining for them since they were gone. At worst, it'll all have been a huge waste of energy because: a) the story they've uncovered isn't close enough to the truth, or b) their birth mother fears the breakdown of her new family if she connects, or c) their birth mother is dead, or scenarios d through z.

THE "UNKNOWN" CULTURE CLUB

I believe in my new hospital ground story as a default, but I have no faith in it. It may bring me closer to the truth, or it may take me further away. The closest I've gotten to uncovering my birth story is through a connection with a fifth cousin I made on 23andme—the genetic testing program. I've found a really nice Korean family who resides in Australia. They believe me to be the daughter of their fifth cousin who lives in Korea. If it's true, my Korean father's girlfriend—my birth mother—took off with me. However, when they visited Korea, they were unable to confirm this. And even if it's true, I still don't know how I ended up in Daegu at the White Lily Orphanage, or if it was via the hospital grounds.

You can give a child a new name, new paperwork, and a new family and hope for the best. I know I was more fortunate than many who ended up in horrifically abusive families. And for that, I feel grateful and guilty.

Some adoptees have no desire to know the life that came before their adoptive families. I used to be one of them. But for the rest of us, there will always be that nagging tug of questions that we wish didn't have to be there.

While I'm not all for transracial adoptions, I'm also not entirely against them. I view them as a last resort to a failed system. I believe in supporting the family within their birth country, followed by adoption within their own country, followed by fostering within their own country—so the child can grow up with reflections of themselves, in their own culture, feeling a sense of belonging. This doesn't mean that I wish I were never adopted, or that I resent my own family—lest I be viewed as ungrateful. I believe there's a place for adoption, that there really are some unwanted babies, and that those babies deserve the next best shot at loving homes. But I don't believe all of us who were adopted were simply unwanted.

As I age and further educate myself on these matters, I simply can't turn away from countless realities in order to continue to praise adoption and the savior mentality. I don't believe that if we all weren't adopted, we would be dead, prostitutes, or even homeless. Those stories are told to paint adopters as saintly, and the truth is, not all adopters are worthy of such a pedestal. In fact, most aren't. Adopters are also getting something they want—a child. And that child will not likely maintain the ignorance or gratitude of that of a pet. We will grow from a child into adults with curiosities, skepticism, and complex emotions that stem from our unknown lives before. We deserve to explore our real roots without guilt and assumptions. But mostly, we deserve not to have to spend so much money and time doing so.

The Baby Box, a legally installed hatchet connected to churches usually promoted by religious facilities in the effort to obtain and save infants for adoption, denies those children records to find back the family we are part of and our origin when we reach adulthood. Without the Baby Box, parents are still able to relinquish their children, but are required to provide paperwork that will make it easier for reunion if either party wants it later on.

Statistics show that mothers of adoption-loss have lived in anguish over never being able to trace the children they relinquished—or who were stolen from them, for their own good. On top of that, adoptees spend small fortunes trying to trace and find their Korean families—often to no avail.

Tomorrow is my birthday on one record, however on every other legal documents, such as my adoption papers, driver's license, and passport, March 16th is recorded as my date of birth. For about a decade, and every day in between, I wake up wondering if that day is in fact my birthday, and if there's anyone out there of my own flesh and blood who thinks of me on that day. I wonder what kind of emotions he or she may have and what has been afforded to them because I have been removed.

Sometimes, I think their sadness seeps into me and weighs me down—like somesort of meta-biological connection. And sometimes I just thank being alive and well since it took a long time to feel love and be able to love.

Those who know the day and time they were born as a birth right, along with people who remember that glorious occasion, may find it difficult to understand why a particular day matters so much. "Just use any day," some say, or, "Just be thankful to be alive." Some even refuse to accept another day of our choosing since it is not the date they've always known it to be—it messes with their truth. And to them, I struggle to give a meaningful enough answer that will undoubtedly be just. But every year, it's a reminder of all that I don't know—despite my gratefulness for who I've allowed myself to become, and everyone who's helped me get here. Every year, there's a reopening of a wound that was denied being a wound for so long.

The best thing I can come up with is a need for closure. You hear all these awful stories about missing people and their survivors not knowing if they're alive or dead. There are movies and television series about parents just wanting to know how their child died. There's just something about knowing—even if it's the most awful truth—that's a comfort to some.

I've stated elsewhere that I don't fault the pastor of the Baby Box—who's likely a wonderful man—for doing in his heart what he believes is right. But I do not think it's right. Having a record of your birthdate and who you were born to should be a birth right. Whatever social and political laws that keep us from it, is the failure. And those who charge large fees to "help" us uncover what's rightfully ours—whether they help or not—are atrocious.

In this day and age, we know better from the generations of adoptees and split families before now. How long will people accept this narrative for these poor "discarded" children? And when will people stop profiting from this biased system? For nearly every one of these children, there is a family who would have preferred help to care for their baby, rather than to give the away to chance. Those families deserve more honor and support—dare I say—even more than adopters.

✈ **JESSICA SUN LEE**

16

KILLING ME SOFTLY WITH NO WORDS

In honor of November, which is National Adoption Awareness Month, oh, sing me those blues, Ms. Holiday;

> *"Them that's got shall have,*
> *Them that's not shall lose.*
> *So the Bible said and it still is news.*
> *Mama may have, Papa may have*
> *But God bless the child that's got his own..."*

    I'm looking out of our kitchen window at the first major snowfall of the season as I'm writing, and though it's visually beautiful, there's something about the muffled quiet and the bitter cold of a snowy winter day that puts my mind in a state of solitude and melancholic introspection. This particular day, it reminds me of how alone I am ...
    Alone, because odds are good that I will never know my original family. Alone, because my adoptive family does not get me. *At all.*

Alone, because I'm an Asian face in a predominantly white world, and I'm reminded of that every day.

Alone, because I still feel like I don't have a defined identity.

Alone, because I struggle with accepting people's love.

I have always wondered what I would be like if I didn't have the albatross of adoption around my neck. But the state of being adopted is all I've known. I was the first kid to be adopted in my family, in 1975. Between my immediate and extended family, there are a total of six adoptees. Two from Korea (me included), two from China, and two local.

A few years ago, at a large family gathering, my uncle, who is a pastor, held court after he and my aunt adopted my cousin from China. He waxed philosophic, thanking my parents for starting this "tradition of adoption" in our family. I remember feeling like a human Cabbage Patch Kid with all eyes on me. I wanted to crawl into a hole and not be the family's poster child for starting this "tradition." But instead, I politely nodded in the appropriate places, and didn't say anything. As an adoptee, you feel like you can't say what you're really feeling to your adoptive family. It's a fear of rejection, of not having your feelings validated.

There's also a power imbalance; on some level, I do believe most adoptive parents believe they somehow "saved" their child from some unsavory terrible fate. So as an adoptee, you're always skating that fine line of "gratitude." We were abandoned once, we don't want to risk having our adoptive families abandon us as well (maybe not physically, but emotionally). So we generally keep silent so as not to rock the boat. (Side-note to adoptive parents: Just because your adopted child may not overtly show any signs of emotional or mental duress does *not* mean that everything is peachy-keen within your child.)

For me, keeping silent has been almost deadly. I've struggled with depression most of my life. How it relates to adoption is sort of a chicken or egg thing for me; am I depressed because of the adoption issues, or am I a "natural" depressive who happens to be adopted? I do not know. I've always been creative, emotional, artsy. So perhaps I have the clichéd "artistic temperament" to begin with, which is a somewhat volatile thing in and of itself. I recall having inappropriate emotional outbursts around second grade (interestingly around the same time I wanted my teachers and classmates to call me by my Korean name), so I know this stuff has been with me for a long time.

My first suicide attempt came in eighth grade. I was lonely, and I felt worthless. My grades were suffering for the first time during my entire schooling. I remember having crushes on many girls, but every single one of them rejected me. I was a "nice guy" but only insofar as an arms' length of friendship. I didn't understand how I could be considered funny, smart, talented, engaging, yet be rejected by *everyone*. Adoptees don't do well with outright personal rejection.

Looking back, I think my peers sensed something that I didn't, at least not yet ... one of my nicknames was "Fucked Up Genius." *Talk about a half-compliment!* But home life wasn't much better; constant fighting with my parents coupled with their increasing religiosity didn't make things any easier. One night, I swallowed a bunch of aspirin, but vomited it all up soon after. I remember weeping and thinking, "You're such a failure! You can't even off yourself!"

I have had two other near suicide attempts in more recent times, but you get the idea. How can a person do this to themselves over and over? Well, here are a handful of points that reflect my reality of transracial adoption:

•Whatever the circumstances of your birth were, you feel as though at one point in time *you were not wanted nor loved.*

•Living in a society that sees you as an outsider or fundamentally as the *other*.

•Having an adoptive family that doesn't really care to know who you are, and doesn't want to know, for fear that *they* failed as caregivers.

•Looking at yourself in the mirror and seeing a stranger.

•*Not* being heard ... when you try and talk to non-adoptees, they can't get past their own preconceived notions of what society says adoption should be like. They will argue with you, like they *know* what *being* adopted is like.

These are just a few main points. You may say, "Those seem like setbacks, but enough to kill yourself over?"
Well, imagine each of these points as being a cancer cell. Imagine a lifetime living with these cells, and having each of them root and spread out poisonous tendrils over the entirety of your very soul and being. After a while, you will feel like a trapped animal, and you will crash. *Trust me.*

Happy National Adoption Awareness Month.

✈ JOO, HYUN

17

DUALITY

In writing out my pain about being adopted (which for me is personally defined as the trauma from being separated from my birth mother as an infant, plus the trauma of being separated from a foster mother plus the trauma of being taken out of Korea and sent to the United States plus the trauma of my adoptive mother leaving the family when I was four-and-a half years old, plus multiple moves all before the time I reached twelve years of age, I sometimes feel that when I share this with others, I should attach a disclaimer that states the following:

I can have the following feelings simultaneously. One does not discount or trump the other. These feelings run concurrently and sometimes they intersect and sometimes they simply continue to run parallel as if neither was aware of the other's existence.

1. I hate that I was adopted. I am thankful (not grateful) that I was adopted by a loving family.

2. I would love to know who my Korean mother is. I don't hate my adoptive family.

3. I love being Korean. It was difficult to grow up in a place where I did not fit in.

Korean Adoptees, Then and Now

4. I would love to visit Korea. I have a lot of anger about the news regarding Korea's treatment of single mothers.
5. My adoption made me stronger. My adoption royally fucked me up.
6. I post a lot about my feelings about being adopted. I don't want to be defined solely by my adoptee status.
7. I do harbor some resentment towards Caucasian people who adopt. I don't think that all Caucasian people who adopt are monsters.
8. I have suffered trauma and want to take care of it. I do not blame or see myself as a victim! (Obviously, this is a big one.)
9. I like to be around Korean adoptees because it feels familiar. I'm not a racist nor do I dislike my non-Korean friends.
10. I was abandoned/relinquished/separated from my Korean mother. My adoptive mother's love—while powerful—cannot 'fix' the separation.
11. I was a "happy" child. I believe it's okay if I recall the ways I wasn't happy.

I feel as though the knee-jerk reaction when an adoptee talks or writes or shares feelings about his or her experiences, is to get defensive and to assume that if A is true then B *must* be true as well. This couldn't be further from the truth! Let me share my hurt and anger and frustration and confusion and please withhold your assumptions that I'm *only* angry and hurt and frustrated and confused. This shit is complicated. It's complicated for adults to understand; now take this all and apply it to the fact that when all of this took place in many of our lives, the majority of us were babies or small children and could literally not comprehend much less cope with what was happening to us.

When I write, talk, seek therapy or every so often venture to post in my blog publicly, I am not asking for apologies or pats on the back and I do not want you to feel ashamed or guilty or like you must answer my sharing with a list of reasons why I shouldn't feel the way I do. Sometimes it's ok to simply respond with silence. It really is.

→ KATHRYN LUSTIG

18

REFLECTIONS OF SEOUL

Seoul is the city where my life started. Seoul is known as the city that never sleeps and the city that houses more people than the whole of Sweden. Seoul is the city that has stolen my heart and also has broken my and many of my friends' hearts.

Seoul is the place where you can see beautiful temples and ornate palaces and where you can walk beside the *Cheonggyecheon* stream in the middle of the city. The Han River can be seen in varying lights throughout the day, evening and onward past the night. Every time I cross the Han river, I smile and enjoy its beauty. Seoul is also the place where you can make a close friend with whom you can share your adoption experience and the longing to find your Korean family.

The more time I spend in Seoul, the more I love the city and the more I feel that it is my city. Slowly, step by step, I conquer pieces of it. When I rode in the taxi back to my friend's place, I realized that I started to recognize parts of the area where she lives. Earlier, I had only recognized the area close to KoRoot, a guest house for adoptees. By recognising more areas, I feel that the city of Seoul belongs to me.

Korean Adoptees, Then and Now

Seoul has also caused me so much pain. I see the injustices which seem to never end, where families are torn apart and never meet again, where the old is demolished and forever lost. A place where success is hailed and the imperfect is chased away. Seoul is the place from which many of my friends and I were sent overseas because certain individuals within the Korean government did not recognise our human right to be raised by our own families.

Regardless of how much pain Seoul and some of its citizens have caused me, this is the place where my life began. My history started in a poor area called *Wangshimini*, an area known now as New Town —a place that has been demolished and will be rebuilt—another way to forget the past. The demolishers are unaware of the people's feelings who once lived there—the feelings of us who used to belong to that area.

Today *Wangshimni* is vacant. All I can see when I return is a high wall surrounding what once most likely was my mom's residence. Visiting here makes me feel close to my mum, although deep inside I know that I will not find her even by returning.

Not only do I return to a wall in *Wangshimni*, but also to the old baby hospital where I and so many other overseas adoptees used to stay. The building is the same but the traces of the children who once stayed there before we were sent away are long gone. Still, sitting down outside a building that is now a children's library makes me feel close to the 200,000 Korean children who were not welcomed to stay in Korea.

The third place I stayed during my short life in Seoul is an orphanage in Amsa-dong. This building is long gone too. It's true that Korean family search is not only a race against family member deaths and the destruction of records, but also the destruction and rebuilding of places. Similarly, it's also the complete erasure of collective memory and landscape. Although I rationally know that I cannot recreate what I have lost, I return to the places that once were mine with the vain hope to feel some kind of belonging.

Park Chung Hee's dictatorship and the adoption agency stole my roots when I was a child. Despite this, I love Seoul. Seoul is the city I dream of and long to be in, and at the same time, it's the city I abhor and want to avoid. Although I have lost so much in Seoul, I can't escape from the place where my life started. I can't deny my birthcity. As a consequence, I have chosen to return no matter how painful it is.

✈ **HANNA SOFIA JUNG JOHANSSON**

19

MESSAGE ON COLORBLIND PARENTING

In an article authored by Karen Valby that appeared online on February 12, 2015, on the website of TIME magazine, I was quoted as an adult transracial adoptee, discussing an issue that for a very long time has been a preoccupation of mine: what I and others have referred to as "colorblind" parenting.

Allow me to explain. I am an adult Korean adoptee, born in South Korea in 1960, and adopted as an infant by parents of Norwegian-American and German-American backgrounds, and raised, along with a twin, in Milwaukee, Wisconsin, in the 1960s and 1970s. Though I was raised by very loving, caring parents, I grew up in America in a time and place that exposed me to a great deal of racism, and yet also in a time and place in which neither my parents nor anyone else had access to important concepts, ideas, and vocabulary that could have helped me as a child to understand and integrate my experiences of race and racism. As a result, I spent decades trying to unravel for myself a very complex set of experiences around race and racism.

Having now spent fifteen years in public and semi-public spaces around transracial and international adoption, I have interacted with countless adult transracial adoptees, adoptive parents, and first parents. If there is a single issue that seems to come up more than practically any other around the raising of children adopted transracially, it is around how to "deal with" race.

The majority—perhaps even the vast majority—of white transracially adoptive parents come to this discussion having been raised in white culture and not having been exposed to concepts around racism and particularly white privilege. So even those who are extremely well-intentioned start out disadvantaged as they try to begin to figure out how to "deal with" race, as they raise their children of color.

Yet I can say with absolute certainty, based not only on my own personal experiences in this area, but also based on the experiences of the countless adult transracial adoptees I've met, that race is going to be a core issue in any family created through transracial adoption. And thus, this paragraph introduced me in Valby's excellent TIME article from February 2015:

"Parents who believe they can raise their child color-blind are making a terrible mistake,' says Korean adoptee Mark Hagland, a 54-year-old journalist and adoption literacy advocate. 'And it's shocking how many people I meet still think this way. If there's a single thing I can share with white adoptive parents [it's to] look at the adult adoptees who have committed suicide, or who have substance abuse problems. Love was not enough for them.'"

The fact is that even today—in 2015, as I write this essay—many, many white transracially adoptive parents believe that they can raise their children "colorblind"—meaning that they can simply pretend that their children are white, or "white-like." In other words, they can erase their children's racial identity. Inevitably, those children end up having the experience of racism without the support of their parents, who remain committed to raising their children as though they were white—which they aren't. Every single child of color in U.S. society—and in most societies that are white-majority or white-dominant—will experience racism, and many will experience it regularly or often.

So if there's a single message I have for white transracially adoptive parents, it is this one: please, please, please learn about race, racism, and white privilege, and do not for one moment believe that you can raise your children successfully in the way that you were raised, as a white person in a white-dominated society.

THE "UNKNOWN" CULTURE CLUB

It won't work, and your children will spend decades, as those of us in the earliest waves of transracial adoption have done, unraveling the very difficult contradictions in their childhoods.

✈ **MARK HAGLAND**
Excerpt from My Message To Transracially Adoptive Parents About "Colorblind" Parenting: Don't Do It.

PART FOUR:

"UNKNOWN" FUTURE

20

I CAN'T KEEP GOING NOT KNOWING

One evening, I was sitting on the couch, sobbing and missing my husband, struggling with emotions on my own, fighting to become a citizen, having a blah night. I got online and wanted to know: *How to find answers as to why I'm the only person in this world that's having this crap for a life.* I was thinking: "why at this time—when all other American women retire and slow down with the safety of social security—am I fighting to prove I exist?" I am sixty-one years old. I've lived in the United States for more than fifty years. I've honestly paid into the system! That's when I started looking for answers. I keyed in: "adoptive children and the real truth." What came up was "Adoption Truth and Transparency Worldwide Network Group." I asked to join and found others like me.

✈

Only six months ago my husband died. We were married for almost thirty-three years. He spent the last three years living in a hell of sorts that included surgery to stop his brain from bleeding caused by a doctor who administered too much blood thinner. I didn't leave his side the entire time he was in hospice. For the last three years I cared for him. He got confused at times and I watched him constantly; he was like a small child because he wandered off on occasions. He also survived a hip replacement caused from falling. These traumatic events were his last straws—he just gave up and died.

At the age of sixty, immediately after his death, the Social Security Office told me, "You are not a US Citizen. Therefore you are not eligible for widow's benefits."

"*What?!*" The news just turned my whole world upside-down. My husband paid into the Social Security system his whole working life. And I paid into the system for thirty years! My parents were American citizens when they adopted me in 1955, they were Americans when they died, and I was told I was an American citizen throughout my entire American life since the age of two! Now who am I and where do I belong? To which country do I look to for the end of my life? The only document I have is an old passport from 1956. I haven't seen any other adoption documents. I don't even know if any papers about me exist!

At the age of sixty-one, I am now trying to obtain US Citizenship. I worked the majority of my life, which included jobs as a cosmetologist, an electrician inside a nuclear plant and even in an army base before and after the 9/11 attack. We paid our taxes and paid into Social Security: my husband for forty years and myself over thirty years. I've got to figure out what and who the hell I am. I always thought I was an American by my adoption and yet here I am finding out somebody did not complete the paperwork!

I am now going through this turmoil alone not knowing what my future holds. If my application for citizenship is not accepted, I will once again be a street child and may be deported to Korea. This time, thrown into a foreign country as an elderly street person. How does one become a foreigner in two countries? One nation gave me to another as a minor child and I had no choice in the matter. And then, to find out sixty years into the future that I was never considered a legal citizen by the adoptive country? How is this in the best interest of children?

I have to prove my citizenship and legal marriage to the United States authorities. For my adoptive parents to not complete my adoption is just one more cruel abuse they have inflicted upon me. How many other adopted people are going to find themselves in this position or already have? How many intercountry adopted adults are living as Americans, believing wholeheartedly that they're Americans—paying taxes and social security as my husband and I did only to find out late in life that we are not legally citizens and this non-status is held against us?

At the time of my adoption, neither the Seventh Day Adventist Church stationed in Korea, nor my adoptive parents finished my citizenship papers. The home I was at in Korea was named Seoul Sanitarium and Hospital, and it was founded by a doctor and his wife who also owned and operated an orphanage. This makes me feel like I was kidnapped! Finding out my noncitizen status is even more mind-blowing after losing the one person who stood up for me—my husband.

Back in the mid-fifties, my adoptive mother wanted two boys because she favored her biological son but not her daughters. My adoptive father would not sign the papers unless she agreed to take a *girl and a boy* because he was raised in a family of sisters and brothers. According to Dad, raising two boys would *not* be a normal family—he wanted a daughter. My adoptive mom finally agreed, but the agency sent the girl my adoptive parents fell in love with to another household and sent me instead. The agency expedited my adoption papers, so that they could send me, a replacement child, out of the country and into the arms of strangers. I am not even the original child my adoptive parents agreed upon! I also served as a replacement for my adoptive mother's biological daughters who chose to live with their father when my adoptive mother divorced and remarried.

At the age of two-and-a-half, I was brought to the United States to be given a better life—as they told me almost daily. I have had my nationality and culture stripped from me, I have faced bullying all through school because in America if you had different-looking eyes and skin color you were ridiculed and called chink, slant eye, or yellow skin.

I was "touched" by my adoptive father and members of the church. My father drove a truck and he would take me on trips with him. As early as age four, I can remember being terrified of the rain, storms, wind and that I would rather shake in bed than find help. I remember blood. I remember being awakened by him fiddling with me. I remember being whipped with some sick twisted sexual quirk. I remember being stripped down until I was buck naked and arranged across the bed. When the whipping was over and I didn't move, my adoptive father whacked me ten to fifteen times. If I moved, he whacked me another ten.

When we returned home from these horrible trips, my adoptive mother called me a whore. I think there is a pattern for adoptive mothers of a different race to react with jealousy against their adoptive daughters. From as young as ten years old, I can't remember not being touched in a way a young girl should not be. Male members of the church—including some higher up elders—sexually abused me, which got worse at age fourteen.

I was a slave to behave and act like my adopter's child. You know, like a pet. Except usually animal owners don't enter their little doggy's room at night to do nasty things. And then, because the new pet responds differently than the owner expected it to (it's not completely submissive), they throw the puppy out of their so-called loving forever family. They get tired of the pup growling every time they hurt it. They really have better things to do than to raise a small creature they promised to love and care for. Actually a pup they kidnapped since they didn't even respect it enough to finalize its adoption papers. As a result, later on in its life, the puppy's life becomes a scrambled mess. She isn't a citizen in the foreign country she was kidnapped into. Unless she can obtain citizenship, at the age of 61, she loses all the benefits she's earned throughout her life.

Are you wondering how anyone could be so cruel to a dog? Are you glad your state has laws that make it illegal to abandon animals? Do you think you could never hurt a small animal like that? I bet most adoptive parents hadn't planned to be this cruel when they applied for a child via the adoption process. I also bet they would deny any wrong-doing because they tried to raise the pup according to their Bible. Would you be horrified if someone harmed or terrorized a pup? Truthfully, this is a metaphor based from my adopted life after being taken from Korea as a little human being.

THE "UNKNOWN" CULTURE CLUB

I see many people who love animals but can hurt children. I find this behavior peculiar. So much money is spent to love animals, taking them to doctors, setting up laws to ensure the pet isn't abandoned or tortured, feeding them expensive food, yet they can take children into their house and beat them until they bleed. All in the name of, I adopted you because I love you. They then earn more stars in heaven and the public falls in love with their actions so much, that even the child's voice goes completely ignored—even into adulthood as an adult adoptee.

Children are not of legal age at the time of their adoptions to even sign paperwork, nor are they ever told they need to get their status within the receiving country legalized. The majority of Americans didn't want to see our yellow skin and slant eyes. The Korean War was too fresh in people's minds. They lost sons, husbands, fathers, all reason for people to turn a blind eye toward the abuse inflicted upon small Asian children. The adoptive parents were adamant about scolding us over our status as adopted people. We better appreciate our status: they took us off the streets of Korea and gave us a good education. We were told this so we wouldn't tell their dirty little secrets. Just the fact that we were told this nonsense makes international adoption ugly.

I attended a private Christian school and secluded summer camps. Some aspects were good but many bad facets overshadowed the good. I was kept inside such a small group of people that you don't see a true picture of the outside world. Then, as a teenager, I start seeing a realistic picture. I discovered my secluded community was not even close to reality. Was this isolation enforced purposefully so that the adopted children refrained from talking about what goes on in adoptive families?

I'm beginning to wonder if my adoptive mother knew of my circumstance—that if she didn't fill out the paperwork, I could be deported. At age sixteen, she sent me to Juvenile Hall, in a psychiatric ward and a boarding school. Even though I was married at the time, she sent this message on my eighteenth birthday: "I hope they deport her," referring to me—the girl she adopted to be her daughter! Most hurtful was that she hoped that I would be deported to live on the streets of Korea! After the birth of my daughter, she refused to visit us. How can we not expose this in-

Korean Adoptees, Then and Now

justice even if it means holler, scream, kick and, if necessary, hold pickets or whatever it takes to be heard?

When you are rejected by the only family you know as a teenager, you start fighting. You have no resources. You are scared-to-death that at any moment you could end up on the streets. You see, the threat was always: "If you don't obey, we will send you back."

My own adoptive dad foresaw my predicament. Just before his passing, he told my husband and me: "An adopted child can't be deported. Check with Washington."

I did not understand and just blew it off, not wanting to think about what I felt he could be implying.

Because I was not a birth child, I got treated differently and I don't care what anybody says, I see more and more evidence of this against other children: There is no way I will ever be convinced that people can treat an adoptive child just like a birth child.

"You do realize you might not be Korean." My aging adoptive mom told me while I fed her in the nursing home. "You might be Mexican."

I responded, "Well, the passport you gave me is in Korean."

She answered, "Well who knows. It might not be real."

For forty plus years, I did not know who, or what or where I came from, but I do remember the threat: "If you don't behave, you will be sent back."

I am learning about many adoptive parents who do not treat their adoptive children like they first agree. Then, the children are left out of the will as legal heirs. Rather, the natural children are left everything. The birth children take their inheritance and leave. And, we adoptees, end up taking care of our adoptive parents.

The roadways to intercountry adoption were built and cemented as recently as after the Korean War and then the Vietnam War. People realized children could be commodities to sell, like registering puppies. Nowadays, they find vulnerable families and make it appear as if they will help but realistically they steal away the child for a profit. Until I got online, I didn't realize how many people were paid for taking in children. I knew about the church deal: that church members could appear noble for taking in children and get that special pat on the back: Atta boy.

How can you reform kidnapping?

A lot of us adoptees were well-trained to keep the dirty little secret. I am now in my sixties. Until the very last few years of my life, I would not speak of how I truly felt about adoption. If I did, my childhood training took over: I might be at risk of being sent back. When threatened this much as a small child, I would not risk telling the truth.

Real adoption issues need to be brought to light. I am possibly facing deportation. If I am not granted citizenship or if I do not get my social security benefits, I will end up homeless. I ask again: is international adoption in the best interest of the child? I still wonder what will happen to me? And what will happen if I stand up for something?

We, intercountry adoptees, were kidnapped victims who were abused then sent way or denied our rights by that same factor that we were removed—not of our own free will—to lifelong lives away from our homeland.

Today, I am trying to be the legal widow of the man I married thirty-three years ago and get the social security we both paid into. Angry? *You bet.* Wanting the world to know it? *Hell, Yeah.* Ready to holler, "It ain't right." *You got it.* Yes, I get crazy now. *I can't keep going much longer not knowing.*

✈ **KIM YANG AI aka "E"**

I TRULY BELIEVE THEY WERE MY FAMILY

All I wanted was to be the best American I could be. The shock of my life happened on January 30th, 2015 when the United State's Department of Homeland Security served me with deportation paperwork.

My name is Adam Thomas Crapser. In the spring of 1979 and at the age of four, I was adopted with my biological sister and another Korean girl from the same orphanage, to the United States. We were sent to the state of Michigan to be adopted by Stephen Michael and Judith Wright. This Lutheran couple gave me the name of Adam Richard Wright. The Wrights had five biological children, three girls and two boys, ranging from infant to mid-teens. During this initial time of our adoption, I really believed that they were our family.

During these approximate five years with the Wrights, we were subjected to many forms of physical and sexual abuse. My earliest memories at this house included violence and fighting—stuff I wasn't used to at the Korean orphanage. My sister and I fought back the best we could and she stood up for me a lot. This household would be my first memories of major violence and dysfunction. We didn't assimilate into this family very well and I've tried to block out the physical abuse and trauma from both of them. I learned many years into the future that the Wright's son was sexually abusive toward my biological sister.

My biological sister and I lived with the Wrights, our first set of adoptive parents, for about six years until March 21, 1986 when they were preparing to divorce. Eventually, they relinquished us to the Children's Services Department of the state of Oregon and separated. I didn't know where they took my sister. For almost two years until October of 1987, I lived in foster, shelter care, and boys homes, such as the Perry Center for Children in Portland, Oregon, where there was more abuse which was also hard to understand while growing up.

In June of 1989, I was then formally adopted a second time to a couple named Thomas and Dolly-Jean Crapser who were devout Jehovah Witnesses. The couple met at a Midwest traveling carnival during the 60s. They had three biological boys, two of which were older and did not live in the home with the two other legally adopted children and me. They gave me a new middle and last name of Thomas Crapser. Over the next few years, there would be four foster children who would be assigned to live there. We ranged in ages from six to thirteen years old.

The only thing I wanted was a family, and I thought this couple would be my real parents. Most of all, I wanted to be loved and to be reunited with my sister.

I was bullied incessantly because of my stature, my eyes, my ethnicity, my last name, and the fact that I was adopted. I was the only Asian child in elementary and middle school, and because I was quite a bit smaller than the other kids, I dealt with severe bullying. After a while, I had to stick up for myself. My adoptive father was an old school type of guy and his advice to me was, "double up the fist and punch 'em in the mouth."

At home, it seemed as if one of us children would be choked, beat, hit or burned—some form of heinous sadistic abuse—every day. My adoptive father broke my nose at the age of fourteen because I couldn't find his car keys. These would be some of my memories of brutality, torture, neglect and hopeless terror. Just to name a few incidences stated by the deputy district attorney for the county after a two and a half month investigation, we endured, "gagging and beating, striking on the head with a clubbing device, hitting with a belt, kicking, shoving against a wall," reported by The Seattle Times.

At age fourteen, I committed two acts of assault which included a fist fight involving braces and another involving five other guys and homemade nunchucks in an attempt to protect myself. For this I was charged and pled guilty to assault and juvenile detention and placed on probation.

June 4th of 1991, the Keizer Police and other agencies came and removed myself and seven other children from the Crapser home. My adoptive parents were charged with at first seventy counts of different forms of abuse, including child rape and sex abuse. The following day, the Crapsers' biological son and I ran back to the home. My life was falling apart again and I did not understand what was going on.

My parents were eventually charged with 34 counts of rape, sexual abuse and criminal mistreatment of us. They plea-bargained and Mr. Crapser was convicted of child rape, child sex abuse, child abuse, and criminal mistreatment. His punishment was jail for 90 days, a $5000 fine, and two years on probation. He did have to register as a sex offender but is currently taken off the registration today and his name can't be found by the public. Mrs. Crapser was convicted on two counts of assault and three counts of criminal mistreatment and given a suspended ninety day jail sentence and two years probation.

Tom Crapser paid over $150,000 to his attorney who represented him. The state appealed the sentences, requesting twenty years for Tom Crapser and ten years for Dolly Crapser but was not successful. The case was covered by local news and media and I faced more bullying from peers and ex-classmates. As a consequence, I dropped out of school and managed to get my GED.

The only thing I wanted was a family. I wanted them to care for me and love me and to reunite me with my biological sister. Instead, I was always told to stop worrying about Korea and my birthmother because I was American now. No attempts were made to connect me with my biological sister.

After many arguments and fights, the Crapsers kicked me out of the house at age sixteen and I became homeless. I worked at three fast food joints and slept in a car. It was the first time I truly felt hopelessness and despair. I experimented with drugs and even contemplated suicide. I had to learn how to take care of myself. I learned many things about myself and life at this age. I didn't have much growing up, never got naturalized by my adoptive parents, but I did the best I could. I really believed that the Crapsers were my true family—the only family I really had.

At the age of seventeen, I broke a window to get into my adoptive home so that I could retrieve my Korean Bible and rubber shoes—things I had asked for over the years which came with me from the Korean orphanage. I was unsuccessful. My adoptive parents refused to return my belongings—including my birth certificate, my adoption records and they didn't help me with my naturalization—they kept these things from me or just threw them away. I felt inside-out most of my life because for the longest time, I felt like I was the only one.

After I turned eighteen, I was charged with burglary in the first degree. The Crapsers, as well as the state's Public Attorney, convinced me to take the plea bargain for eighteen months probation. I agreed, was prosecuted and charges were filed against me.

Because of my juvenile assault convictions and sentencing to twenty-five months in the 1995 Oregon Department of Corrections, I was upward departed on the Oregon sentencing grid and sent to prison. This was the first interactions I had with other Asians. I just didn't know what to think. The environment was different than county jail. I was confused going in.

Upon release I was allowed to stay at the Crapsers property in a trailer for thirty days but was kicked out again for not following Dolly Crapsers' rules to attend the Kingdom Hall, a Jehovah Witness Church. In our younger years, if we didn't attend we would be punished by pinching, hair pulling and spankings.

After prison, I was homeless again and making bad choices but gaining some street-smarts. I stayed anywhere I could and even went to the Salvation Army and Union Gospel Mission's, Men's Shelters. I learned how to steal cars in order to pay bills but ended up going back in prison for nineteen months because of those choices.

During this time, I was also being threatened by the Crapsers second oldest son, a very big guy in stature who stood six feet four, weighed 280 pounds and served many years for assault. He threatened me because of the previous break-ins into his parents house. I carried a gun with me at all times in the effort to feel protected, and eventually was charged and pled guilty to Felon in Possession of a Firearm, unauthorized use of a motor vehicle and theft. In 1997, I was sentenced to serve nineteen months. While serving my time, I told myself I didn't want to live this kind of life anymore. The quote, "Get busy living or get busy dying," from the movie *Shawshank Redemption*, stuck with me. I wanted to live.

To try to earn a living, I enrolled in barber training, and continued to attend a community college. After 2001, it was very hard for me to obtain legal employment without lying about my citizenship status. I did, however, maintain employment throughout the years in the automotive and cosmetology fields. I worked as an independent contractor, or under the table many times. I also went on to open a small barber shop and work for myself.

Throughout the course of fifteen to twenty years, I would ask the Crapsers for any and all of my adoption records or information pertaining to my adoption so that I could get a job or go to college. I was denied. For years I was told there was nothing, and that they could do nothing. Because of privacy concerns, they could not get into any sealed records. The Crapsers, in particularly, Tom Crapser, appeared very clever and maintained his reputation in the community. On more than one occasion I have asked my parents over the years why they never naturalized me, and was always told that it was not their responsibility, but I believe they chose not to naturalize me.

During the next sixteen years, I would work, go to school, have a child and try to maintain some semblance of a "normal" life. I told myself that I would be the biggest loser in the world if I went back to prison, so I did the best I could to be honest, pay my bills and stay out of trouble.

There were a few times when I was in the wrong place at the wrong time, and I did end up with two misdemeanor theft charges. In the state of Washington, I was charged and pled guilty to assault three domestic violence with an ex-roommate in August of 2013. I feel that I was forced into pleading in this case. I was sentenced to 366 days and served eight months and twenty days in the Washington State's Department of Corrections. In 2012, I was finally able to apply for a permanent Resident Investigation, which is what triggered my enlistment into the Deportation Proceedings and led to being served deportation papers on January 30th, 2015.

Currently, I have a great family: a five-year-old stepchild, a one-year-old, and a child due in May. I am also accountable to my oldest child who is fourteen and lives in Oregon with his mom. Deportation would displace not only me, but also my family. It would create strain and drain on my wife and children and I don't know if we would be able to survive the separation. It would be major trauma for us, and would victimize my children—honestly the family I have created is of paramount importance to me. I live through my children who have their whole life in front of them. It would drastically impact our family.

If I could say anything to politicians, I would beg them—implore them—to please amend the Child Citizenship Act of 2000 so that those of us who were adopted as children before then but were not granted US citizenship—would finally be covered. Please do this for my children, so they don't have to be ostracized and so our family can remain intact.

All I wanted was to be the best American I could be.

✈ ADAM CRAPSER

22

I DID NOT EXIST IN THEIR DATA BANK

According to my adoption papers, I was found with my umbilical cord still attached to my little five-day-old body on the steps of Daegu City Town Hall on January 22, 1967. That would be in the harsh cold winter of Korea. It seems, I was in poor health and looked downtrodden and disheveled. Some kind soul must have taken pity on me and took me to the White Lily Orphanage. I do not know when I was born. I only found out from my adoption papers that I was received by said Orphanage on that date and no details were attached to me. No name. No birth date. Nothing.

As was the custom at the time, I was given the surname of, Picard, the person who had found me, or so, Sister Teresa of White Lily Orphanage told me, during my first return to Korea in November of 2011. Before I was adopted, I stayed in Korea for almost four years, then sent to Luxembourg in September of 1970, as one of the first adoptees to be received by the small Grand-Duchy, located smack in the centre of Europe.

The people of the village I ended up in, had never even seen an Asian before in their lives. I was a curiosity, to be sure. Prodded and at the same time, "oohed" and "ahhed" over as if I were some exotic, strange and odd creature from another planet. It was unusual to be the only Asian and I felt probably more out of place than I consciously remember. I *do* remember, that even as a child, I had this intense longing for another place, another time, another ...something... I do not know if my ability to remember a previous life (that, curiously enough, I had lived in Asia) had anything to do with my path, or whether it was a way to try and escape a reality that was not easy to deal with on my own at the best of times and nigh too much to deal with in the hardest of times.

My adoptive mother, who I am no longer in touch with at the time of this writing, used to tell me that upon my arrival, and for three months in a row, I would cry myself to sleep every night. As I grew older (around the age of five), She said I hit my head in fury and would throw temper tantrums, dropping myself on the floor, kicking and screaming. I also remember that I had a fury and white rage inside that was eating away at me for the longest time, even after I had outgrown the 'Young and Restless' Sturm and Drang period of my youth.

I was adopted by a dysfunctional couple. My adoptive father being apparently infertile and my mother, desperately wanting her own child, fell 'in love' with me at first sight upon seeing a picture of my sad and distraught face in the catalogue of children available for adoption.

My adoptive father abandoned the family home when I was nine years old, and my adoptive mother, who had no skills, no education and no diplomas, had to start looking for work while at the same time having to care for a 'difficult' and at times 'impossible' child (as she would never fail to remind me). To this day, she tries to use me as her outlet for all her pent-up unresolved issues, mental, emotional and otherwise, especially her anger towards my philandering, spend-thrift and chronic alcoholic adoptive father who ended up dismissing me as his "daughter," and, at a later stage, would cross the street when he'd see me in town or walk right past me in a café. It took me a long time to accept that all my unresolved issues culminated in my nervous breakdown in 2008, when I was told by employees at Holt International that I did not exist in their database.

THE "UNKNOWN" CULTURE CLUB

By then, my relationship with my adoptive parents had completely disintegrated. My father had died in March of 2005 in a fit of a Parkinson crisis, possibly a consequence of his lifelong chronic abuse of alcohol. By the time he died, he had not been a part of my life for over twenty-five years. If at all, I saw him four or five times at most since he'd left the family house. I had serious difficulties of cutting loose the ties with my adoptive mother and I could not deal with her emotional blackmailing, her never-seeming efforts of trying to make me completely and utterly dependent on her for my well-being, while at the same time trying to mold me to her liking by forcing me into mental health facilities and sending me from one shrink to the next, just so I would 'function' according to her idea of a well-adjusted citizen. And, when upon attempting to do my Birth Family Search, Holt Oregon told me that I did not exist in their database, it was as if someone had told me that I had never been born, that I did not exist, that I was totally 'erased'. It triggered a genuine crisis. I thought I was going to completely lose it. The pain, the anger, the hurt, the sense of betrayal on multiple levels, of not just from my own adoptive parents, but my own mother who had relinquished me, the Korean government who had sent me to this dysfunctional couple, Holt who was so cold, unhelpful and impersonal - everything came crashing down on me and I felt as if I'd never recover from the nightmare my life had become.

It is not as if I never would have had some good moments worth recounting. It was only at that moment, time seemed to stand still and I imagined myself disappearing into an abyss of darkness, of a never-ending bottomless pit of pain, despair, blind rage, and hopelessness at the futility of it all. I might as well never have been born.

And yet, in spite of all my demons, my inner turmoil, my sense of not knowing where I belonged, my endless quest for answers, which led me to venture off to live in America and England for four years at a time (though America, being what it was at the time, I could only ever stay three months in a row, leave for one or two weeks and then re-enter with a tourist visa), I continued on my path to experiment with matters that were, what would be considered, outside the five senses, beyond the purely rational, logical or material level of relating to our immediate environment. I continued to explore different ways of meditation, of consciousness and of interpreting reality. I had started to study astrology from the age of twelve, and from sixteen years of age and onwards, numerology, Zen Buddhism, practicing chakra meditations, finding out about color, Bach flower remedies and aroma therapy as well as other alternative healing methodologies in an attempt to find relief from my pain, my longing for a real family, my nagging doubts and, in particular, this dark black hole that was the huge question mark of who I was, who my real family (as I referred to them), my Korean ancestors, my parents and my siblings, my invisible family really were.

Ultimately, that crisis, the nadir of my life, led me to delve deeply and irrevocably towards that which has become my life purpose and my life mission: to heal myself first and then to extend, what I know and have learned over the years across three different continents, to fellow Korean adoptees as well as other transracially adopted peers, and, our white brothers and sisters, who suffer just as much as we do, even if they are spared the pain of losing their culture, language, roots, cultural identity and sense of belonging. I know today, looking back on one of the triggering instances that can be directly connected to my own relinquishment, was that I became unexpectedly pregnant in 2002. The reason, as strange as that may appear, was that I did not even have 'proper' intercourse, and yet, his seed had found its way. I was totally taken by surprise because I had never had a strong desire for children and actually thought, I was infertile because I had had a few close calls, and nothing ever had come of it.

I was living in Los Angeles at the time, on a tourist visa. I had no stable work situation and the father to be was eight years my junior. This young man (I was thirty-six at the time) was the youngest of five children, and had broken ties with his family of Mormons (Latter Day Saints). When he was fifteen years old, his very own mother told him to his face that she wished he had never been born. At the 'ripe' old age of twenty-seven, he had survived a heart attack induced by an overdose of cocaine and alcohol. So, the moment I realized that I was indeed pregnant, there was no hesitation on my part. It was as clear-cut as could be for me: there was no way I was going to have someone's child who had repeatedly told me that he did not want any kids and, in addition, had too much resemblance in his addictive personality make-up to my adoptive father. I did not want that DNA to be passed on to my child and I did not want my child to have to go through what I had to go through as I myself was an emotional wreck. I was not even anywhere close to being able to care for another dependent and helpless human being. I knew that I would absolutely hate myself if I did to my child what my adoptive mother had done to me. So the decision was not even an emotional decision. It was immediate. Right there and then, when I found out, about a half hour before said co-creator was about to pick me up for our date. I never told him until after I had the abortion. I was completely on my own in Los Angeles, not knowing anyone and, all my adoptive mother could think of to tell me over the long-distance phone call was: "How could you be so stupid? What about STDs and AIDS?"

Three weeks after my procedure, I sensed the spirit of my unborn child and I knew it was a boy. It took me about five years until I had resolved my abortion with the help of shamanism and the vine referred to as Mother Ayahuasca, a powerful and potent Amazonian brew concocted of two plants, that has been used by the indigenous peoples of the Amazon for millennia all over the Amazon basin as a means for healing, hunting and curing illnesses, including spiritual malaise of all kinds.

In the summer of 2008, things escalated and I ended up in a hospital because I had tried to commit suicide by swallowing a few too many pills. I had prepared myself as much as possible. I lowered the blinds, and even waited to have processed my digestion having read a few too many accounts of the deceased emptying the remains of their undigested food after their passing and making a mess of themselves, their clothes and wherever they happened to be found.

I had applied to receive an inpatient stay at a clinic in Germany and the answers had been slow in coming. I finally lost it and when things didn't move and there seemed to be no progress in getting admission, I took a desperate step.

In hindsight, I do realize that it was a cry for help and yet, I was so tired of fighting, trying so hard to be heard and seen. The culmination of my failed existence, of feeling lost, dispensable and like a burden to the world, my adoptive mother and myself, nearly drove me over the edge. My adoptive mother had always downplayed my issues, my feeling of being 'out of place' and all she ever had managed to drive home with me was to tell me that I was "too much," "impossible" and just unbearable. Moreover, she tried to sabotage my attempts at self-healing and only wanted me to heal as she saw fit.

When I realized that she would never really want me to fully get well and have a happy life, I decided to cut ties with her for good. To this day, I do not like that woman and no longer speak to her, but I have come to have some measure of compassion for her own history.

My recovery has been slow and it has taken a long time to put everything into perspective but during all that time, my interest in healing, and, especially self-healing, has never subsided. I had not been in a relationship since 2007 and I'd stopped working full time because I was constantly sick from 2004 onwards.

In addition to my physical illnesses, my mental and emotional fragility made working under any kind of normal circumstance or environment a nigh impossibility so I applied for disability pension which was granted to me in 2010. It was as if a burden was taken off my back because I frankly could not deal with anything. I just wanted to be left alone. I could barely make it through the day. In my constant efforts to self-heal, I continued to explore the alternative healing methodologies and drinking *ayahuasca* every few months in conjunction with my 'normal' therapy sessions.

In 2010, I began to have dreams about an elderly Asian woman. Fleeting images of her would come to me in my dreams and I did not know what to make of it, except, I knew she was Korean. She would come in my shamanic journeys with *ayahuasca* as well, yet, I wasn't sure what to make of it. I had yet to visit Korea since my adoption. I had been pulled back and forth between hating Korea for having sent me to my terrible fate and this horrible adoptive couple, and wanting to return to Korea and it was only

THE "UNKNOWN" CULTURE CLUB

because a very kind, supportive and truly empathetic Korean adoptee, James Rosso, who at the time was the Secretary General of GOA'L, the only adoptee organization created and run by adoptees for adoptees located in Korea, kept talking and encouraging me to come out and visit the country of my forefathers that I finally plucked up the courage to apply for GOA'L's First Trip Home in 2011—*and only because I was told that I would be accepted.* As much of a nervous wreck that I was, peculiarly enough my spirits, who had been with me since the late 90s, told me that all would go well.

I was on the KBS program, "I Miss that Person," but to no avail.

In spite of all my attempts to heal any which way I could, and in spite of understanding where my issues had their origin, I still felt out of place, lost and not sure what to do with my life. So in 2012, through an acquaintance, I found a German-Argentinian shaman who, after three soul retrievals, told me that I was to learn to travel shamanically without the use of *ayahuasca*.

Even though I had resistance, I relented and began the training. During my very first soul retrieval with my (future) shamanic teacher, she told me, that it was my maternal grandmother who had saved me from certain infanticide, that it was her who had given me the first and only sense of truly being loved for my own sake and that she felt guilty and devastated that I'd ended up with such a bad family in Europe, and, that if she would have known better, she would have done it differently. And that she had passed away a few years ago.

Yet, it was and is my path to learn to accept and embrace my destiny because it is what has set me on this road to help others who have experienced the same traumas and heartbreak, the same problems and difficulties as I have, to help them heal because I have walked in their shoes and I know what it is like, how difficult it is, what the challenges and pitfalls are.

In December of that same year, 2012, while still in training as a shaman, I was told by my spirits that I should travel to Korea, find an authentic *Mudang* and get a Korean shamanic *hanbok*. I also felt that my maternal grandmother, who I'd never met, 'called' me, and that it was her who I had seen in my dreams and during my shamanic journeys.

Things just unfolded magically and everything fell into place and worked out perfectly in the time frame I stayed in Korea. And even though I do not speak Korean anymore, through some wondrous help from my spirits, and, I felt, my grandmother watching over me, orchestrating the right people at the right time from above, I managed to find a genuine *Mudang* who never asked a penny of me, and who told me that I derive from a long line of female shamans.

My path has continued and is continuing to unfold, and also includes passing on forgiving our parents, whether it is the first or the second or, in some cases, third families. It is only in forgiveness that we can begin to make space for letting go of the pain and the hardship we have had to endure and that we have survived at a great cost of our own well-being, but also, grant forgiveness to our first parents who often did not know any better what to do or were utterly uninvolved in the relinquishment of us at the moment of our being given up. I keep expanding my training in healing methodologies, and have included family constellation work, and now Matrix Energetics, which is based on the quantum physics field of morphogenetic interconnectedness, to broaden my healing approach as much as possible to offer it to those who resonate with wanting to heal with this approach and with these tools.

It is my deepest wish that I may offer my abilities, skills and experience to first parents, to Koreans as a people and to my Korean adoptee peers for we are all in this together.

✈ SONJA SUH

23

BORN AT THE AIRPORT

My name is Kim Goudreau and I was born at Kennedy Airport in New York on December 2nd, 1975, when I was nine years old. I became the daughter of Leo Goudreau and Lorraine Paiement Goudreau, the couple who removed my Korean name of Myung Sook from me. From the eyes of a young child, this foreign coupled appeared like a "fat American man and a yellow-haired woman." The first six months of my new life, I lived in Maine of the United States before moving to Quebec, Canada. Many times I have heard the story of my arrival into this world from the moment I began to understand and speak the language of my adoptive parents. The following is my adoptive mother's memories as she relates my "birth" to others:

"When we received her photo, I thought she was a boy because of her shaved head. I called them and told them, "I don't want a boy; I want a girl." When they told me she was a girl, I attached to her instantly. I loved her and waited for her eagerly every day.

She finally came before Christmas, on December 2, 1975. I'd asked Santa Claus to give me a living doll as a Christmas gift. She's my Christmas gift—my very own living doll.

We were given a VIP room. Everyone was excited and talking at the same time. It was noisy. We were crazy while waiting for our children. All the parents recognized their babies had aged a few months since they had seen them only in photographs. Imagine Asian babies who looked all the same with their slanted eyes.

I felt the pain of childbirth when I saw my daughter. It seems that many women feel the pain of childbirth at the arrival of their adopted children. All the parents started crying as soon as they got their babies in their arms—like any parent would after giving birth. Adopting a child is no different than giving birth. You love them as much as you love your biological children, and even more.

The United States Immigration said there was a problem. They discovered we were not United States citizens. They wanted to send my daughter back to Korea because her visa was found null as we were not Americans. I almost lost my mind at the idea of losing my daughter. Leo left us at the bar and went to plead our case. She was so cute. She took a few sips of Seven Up and pinched her nose. All the adults at the bar watched her. One man told me that she was so pretty, he would like to marry her. It made me angry and I told him, "I just got her! Give me a chance to enjoy her for a few years!"

Leo returned and said, "Lorraine, take the little one and run. Go. Hide. Run fast!" He was able to obtain only a one-year visa for humanitarian consideration, but he was still afraid to lose her. We didn't want to lose her. We were like crazy. I ran and hid in the restroom, but she refused to pee.

While we were in a cab heading to another airport, she finally motioned that she needed to pee, so we had to pull over.

The Last Day of Myung-Sook

Soon after Myung-Sook left the airplane, her escort suddenly stopped walking because of an unknown gray-haired woman who approached. It's only when the escort told me, "Good luck" and left that the little girl realized they wouldn't be together during her stay in the United States. Myung-Sook silently followed the gray-haired woman who herself walked in silence. Once they arrived in a room full of people, the old woman left without saying a word.

Myung-Sook recognized the American couple she had seen from the photograph many weeks earlier. A social worker gave her the photo and said this couple would be her new parents. Her initial thought had been: "The yellow-haired woman is well-dressed and pretty but she doesn't look like a mom. She wears too much make-up like a woman who has led a bad life. The American man can't be a dad, he is too fat." She named the couple "the yellow-haired woman and the fat American man".

The yellow-haired woman embraced Myung-Sook, hugged her, caressed her face and arms, clutched her with outstretched arms, and then fondled again her hair, her arms and everywhere while talking nonstop in a strange language. Myung-Sook grimaced and discretely wiped off her cheeks when she had a chance, totally disgusted by the American woman's lips on her cheeks and she hated her smell and her perfume, but the yellow-haired lady continued to fondle and kiss her, calling her Kim-Kimmi, totally unaware of the little girl's sensitivities.

Meanwhile, the babies who had traveled with Myung-Sook were given to other Americans—one baby for two adults. All the adults cried, laughed and spoke robustly at the same time. It was very noisy. The babies sobbed. The noisy Americans left with the babies and the room returned to quiet.

The fat American man hoisted Myung-Sook onto a bar stool, and then he left too. The yellow-haired woman caressed her again while talking to other men at the bar. Myung-Sook heard them saying "cute" and "pretty" a few times and she was given a glass of Seven-Up. She felt embarrassed and uneasy as they stared at her. Trying to avoid their gaze, she took a few sips of the carbonated drink — the first soda in her life. The tingling sensation in her nose felt funny, and she pinched it several times. She almost burped. Still being stared at by the men, she knew they were all talking about her. She avoided their gaze as much as possible while they continued to talk, point and prod. The moment felt surreal, as if a dream.

The fat man appeared again at the bar and said something to his yellow-haired wife. They seemed quite nervous. Myung-Sook sensed their panic. The American woman grabbed her hand and ran fast—so fast the little girl had difficulty following. The woman slid to a stop in front of a door. Inside, several more doors lined the small room. She rummaged through her purse, found a coin, and inserted it into a slot to one of the doors. The door opened to reveal a western-style toilet. Myung-Sook thought: "Americans are crazy. They have to pay to pee! Americans are rich!"

The woman nudged Myung-Sook into the stall, pulled down trousers, and urinated into the toilet right in front of her, causing the little girl to blush. She had never seen an adult undress in front of her in all her life—not even her own Korean parents! She turned her head away and toward the door but driven by curiosity, cast a quick glance at the yellow-haired woman. The poor American was hairy as a monkey! It reminded her of what her older Korean brother had told her to try to make her laugh when he saw her crying: "If you laugh and cry at the same time, hair will grow on your buttocks like monkeys."

At the surprising sight, Myung-Sook thought, "The poor American woman must have often cried and laughed at the same time. Oh no! I too have laughed and cried many times. I don't want to become like a monkey!" Using a body language and making grunting noises, the American woman motioned Myung-Sook to use the toilet. The little girl shook her head. She didn't want to pee in front of a stranger.

At the main airport terminal, the fat American man gave a pink teddy bear for Myung-Sook as soon as he rejoined the two. She had never seen such a toy. To hide her shyness and her distress, she removed her identification bracelets, slipped them over the teddy bear's arms and focused all attention on the bear, while hugging it to her chest. The yellow-haired woman said, "Pierrot" and Myung-Sook understood the words to be its name—a foreign name to her.

THE "UNKNOWN" CULTURE CLUB

The woman wrapped Myung-Sook in thick unusual cloth, a snowsuit, before exiting the airport to cold and dark wintry weather. She felt alone despite being with the two strangers in such an amazing place. The couple flagged down a taxi, then sandwiched the little girl between them in the backseat. The yellow-haired woman sloppily kissed her cheeks nonstop, leaving it moist and sticky from lipstick. From time to time, Myung-Sook wiped away the slobber from her face. The yellow-haired woman's smell, mingled with strong perfume, made Myung-Sook nauseous, but she was too shy to show disgust.

To make the circumstances worse, Myung-Sook needed to go potty. She just couldn't wait any longer. She jiggled and jostled about in the seat, making the adults understand. The yellow-haired woman recognized the commotion and told the driver to stop. While Myung-Sook urinated on the edge of the road, the yellow-haired woman stood over her like an annoyed owner of a precious possession, like a dog at that moment for which she did not want to lose sight.

✈ **KIM GOUDREAU**

24

THE WAKE-UP CALL

On November 27, 2012, I got the wake-up call of my life when I saw *Mercy Mercy* - a documentary about an adopted girl named Masho. A massive scandal about Ethiopian adoptions hit the Danish media when both this documentary and a series of articles in Politiken, a Danish newspaper, about a girl named Amy were broadcasted. Both Ethiopian girls, together with their siblings, were adopted to Denmark. Reports showed that the Ethiopian parents were coerced to give up their children for adoption. The adoptions failed and both girls ended up in Danish institutional care.

I was shocked and had to find out what was really going on. I saw for the first time how the adoption industry practices. They coerced Ethiopian families to obtain children to fill transnational adoption through a profitable legalized system. My mind was filled with questions and I did not know where I could find the answers.

Why did no one know from where the children came? How can children belonging to families be labeled "orphans" and be adoptable through a legalized transnational adoption system? Why are stolen children not returned? Why is contact between parents and children regularly broken? If families lack medicine, why not provide resources instead of using resources to take away their children?

I could no longer suppress all these questions and many more which came to my mind. It dawned on me that I had always been taught to see the world upside down. I learned that identity, family and one's own true past-cannot be replaced without consequences and that, as a human being, I have rights which should have prevented the lies from happening in my own life—but that strong needs and economic forces are constantly at work to defend the desires of others for the idea of adoption. I searched on social media and the only Danish forums on adoptions I could find was Adoption & Samfund (translated Adoption and Society) Facebook group, an organization mainly for adoptive parents and people on the waiting list. I got my second shock! There was no support for or understanding of the Ethiopian families who were torn apart due to adoption industry's unethical methods of obtaining "orphans" to fill the inexhaustible need for adoptable children. In fact, there was no criticism of the adoption system, but rather a strong defense for the adoption idea at all costs—even when families are suffering. And most shocking an attack against the documentary and adopted people such as myself who insisted on getting straight answers from the industry's so-called experts!

✈

I was seven months old according to my adoption file when I was sent to Copenhagen, Denmark, March 1973. My Danish family would tell me the popular myth about me being brought by the stork instead of an actual airplane. Denmark is a relatively small country with much emphasis on being a Dane. This is expressed through the language and anyone who does not speak Danish fluently or speaks it with an accent has been doomed an outsider. In that way it is a very close-minded country with little to no room for any diversity.

I was adopted into a typical Christian working family, but before I could remember my adopters divorced and they both remarried. As a result I have half and step-siblings, but I am the only one adopted. Like many adoptive families, we didn't talk about adoption. My adoptive mother was diagnosed with cancer when I was teenager and died eighteen years ago and due to my adoptive father's choice, I haven't seen him in the last fifteen years.

Throughout my entire life I have experienced a lot of racism, both micro-aggressions and direct racism, but I didn't fully understood the impact before I was an adult and started to inform myself. Discrimination is often not directed at me, but is rather evident when it is communicated through the community. I have been sent to live with people who do not understand the way I feel. The population does not recognize structural racism or often racism at all. They see it as single episodes, similar to how adoption trafficking is seen. They perceive the scandals, such as in India, Ethiopia, and Korea, to be single episodes and not a structural problem.

Finding spaces and other Korean adoptees to discuss racism with has really empowered me. For example, like within the adoption-area, I learned that the intercountry adoption system is racist in itself initiated by white missionaries who wanted to save brown children from their brown families and communities in the effort to proselytize us, assimilate us and make us as white (and acceptable) as possible.

While growing up I did not have anyone to talk with about racism (or adoption). Instead I was led to believe that I was white. When I was a child my adoptive father took me to a Danish doctor who had been in the Korean War to confirm that I might be half white. The doctor confirmed it could be possible since I was taller than average and had freckles. This was supposed to be a good thing. I thought they wanted me to be white so I bragged about the possibility in my teenage years. Turns out my adoptive father and the doctor were wrong. I took a 23andMe DNA test and I'm not white at all. Now I'm embarrassed about that assumption and proud to be Korean.

At the age of twenty-one, I became a mother and it was the biggest experience of my life. Perhaps due to being an adopted, I needed someone who could connect with me genetically and this connection has had a huge influence on me. I try to teach my daughter about the unequal power-structure in society that made my adoption happen, and shapes our lives in Denmark. My daughter, now an adult, is very interested and understands the need for adopted people to fight for our rights. This is a huge support to me.

I have subsequently gained more insight and understanding behind the dynamics of the adoption environment, including the adoption lobby who are carriers of systematic trafficking of children.

I received great help to understand the system from investigator Arun Dohle of Against Child Trafficking (ACT), an organization that protects the rights of families. He has shown great patience to brief me and it was not easy for me to understand all the details and I'm still learning. ACT is the only child rights organization who stood up for the Ethiopian mothers and the adopted children using huge efforts, costs and media attention. With barely any funding at all they represent the parents of eight children who were stolen and adopted to Denmark and brought four of the mothers to the Danish embassy in Ethiopia, seeking help.

ACT, initially led by Civil Servant Roelie Post understands and highlights the conflict between the United Nations Convention on the Rights of the Child (UNCRC) and the Hague Adoption Convention. Ms. Post was assigned by the EU, to protect Romania's efforts to reform their child protection system from 1999-2005 and her work is detailed in a book called *For Export Only: The Untold Story of the Romanian 'Orphans'*. The UNCRC was written in an effort to prevent children from becoming a commercial commodity; the convention regulates and supports child rights, which considers the movement of children to be the very last resort after all other alternatives have been exhausted. The Hague Adoption Convention, however, has created a legalized child trafficking system.

Initially, I was skeptical and then again shocked. How could I have been so blind? How could all those I had trusted to protect my best interests be so ignorant. I could not believe that my picture of adoption as a win-win situation to be false, but there was no way I could reject the evidence so transparently put forth to me.

It made me so upset, sad and angry that I threw myself into the adoption debate when Against Child Trafficking was the only one who would fight for the Ethiopian families who had lost their children for adoption. I offered my help and have since been active at Against Child Trafficking by helping where I can.

I do not understand how the authorities can ignore and continue to violate the UNCRC in Intercountry Adoptions and why this huge issue is not addressed. How can the families and children who are the victims of illegal adoption and child trafficking be so ignored?

At this point I am strongly concerned to learn that Roelie Post who was asked by the EU to defend the UNCRC in Romania, has been referred to establish an unsupported and non-funded private organization and given no resources to combat violations of children's rights within Intercountry Adoptions. This Civil Servant is very experienced and dedicated as documented in Romania, but why is she no longer allowed to be involved with the protection of the fundamental rights of children? Why has Roelie Post had to pay essentially all Against Child Trafficking's operational costs from her own pocket? How can this be legitimized?

The adoption industry however is given massive financial support, prestige as experts, consultants, and advisers, including adoption facilitators, UNICEF and organizations that ignore the articles within the United Nation Convention on the Rights of the Child and instead implement the Hague Adoption Convention in Romania. A regulated market in children is not in accordance with the UNCRC and unworthy to dignified nations such as the nations of the European Union.

I am appalled to learn that the Hague Convention on Intercountry Adoption is defended, instead of the UNCRC which is EU acquis (the accumulated legislation, legal acts, and court decisions which constitute the body of European Union law).

After the *Mercy Mercy* documentary huge suspicions and scandals regarding baby harvesters, illegal adoptions, and even kidnapping by the orphanage Enat Alem came to light. Against Child Trafficking stepped up to help the Ethiopian families who had lost their children to Denmark, and they let me help where I could.

Since the adoption scandals came out in Denmark, the Minister of Social Affairs set up a working group to devise proposals for a revised Danish Adoption Act. There has been widespread criticism of both the form and content of the analysis, which in its design for example didn't ask to take a position on the UN Convention on the Rights of the Child, or the massive suspicions of systematic criminal acts in connection with already completed adoptions.

The concerns and input from the groups and organizations of adult adoptees, critical adopters and first families were ignored, but instead ISS and UNICEF were appointed as experts, to support access to adoptable children.

The analysis didn't address the conflict between the Hague Convention and UNCRC, but instead recommends the Hague Convention, without commenting on the huge problems in details. Furthermore, the analysis didn't investigate the suspicions of the crimes in the adoptions from such nations as Ethiopia and Nigeria.

Thus far, authorities have not taken further reaction to help the families who were victims of illegal adoptions and child trafficking. Even today, ACT and the mothers who did not willingly relinquish their children are still waiting for advise or reaction. This and much more suspicion and criticism has not been illuminated by the Danish authorities.

Instead the Danish government presents a proposal to relax on adoption rules so that future municipalities will find it easier to forcibly adopt children from their parents, because the number of forced adoptions are too low, despite strong criticism and concerns by adopted people of years past. So, now there are forced adoptions in Denmark! Is that in line with the UNCRC? The faulty system has subsequently given rise to my criticism against the adoption lobby, but our questions have been dismissed, and instead adopters huddle in and cultivate the myth that critical adopted people are mentally ill, accused of having problems of severe attachment and guilty of ingratitude. Defending their hunt for children has remained the priority. I have subsequently been informed to remain outside the established adoption system—especially in some adoptees groups themselves who have opened Pandora's Box, after which news of scandals and corruption have filled my daily life. But it was important to understand the scope and level of resources actually being used to preserve and defend the transnational adoption system—including its myths and lies.

The adoptee community in Denmark and also global adopted people have been a huge support and help in my struggle to understand, inform and help adoptees and our first families. As an adopted person and an European citizen, I am deeply concerned about the developments in the area of adoption, both in Denmark, the European Union and worldwide. I write to express my concern about the massive structural violations of the UNCRC found in the adoption system. I have spent a lot of time on this issue, since I became involved as a volunteer in the work of Against Child Trafficking (ACT).

I have had a lot of difficult experiences as an Asian Adoptee in Denmark and I try to cope by being with as many minorities and other adopted people as much as possible. This expansion of horizons that comes from talking to others who have experienced the same has helped me to understand myself much better. The Adoptee community has meant everything to me and my life has taken a whole new direction because of all the hard work other Adoptee activists do now and before I got my wake-up-call. I took my first trip home to South Korea last fall with Global Overseas Adoptees' Link. It was mind-blowing and I regret that I didn't do it before. I'm now planning my next trip to Korea with my daughter and hopefully as soon as possible.

We are many adoptees who are adults now and we have a voice that can no longer be ignored. It would suit the adoptive parents to listen and be good allies.

✈ JIN VILGAARD

25

I CAN'T DO NOTHING AND CALL IT PEACE

The best people are like water. They benefit all things.
And do not compete with them. They settle in low places.
One with Nature. One with Tao
—Lao Tzu

My visit to South Korea has come to an end and I am about to leave for the US to reflect upon my experiences here and on all the friends I've met during the 2004 Korean Adoptee Gathering. Little would I know that this short trip would serve as a catalyst to connect with an entire "unknown" culture—a culture I would spend the next decade engaged in, listening to the experiences of other Korean-born adopted people—people like me who make up a worldwide club of sorts.

South Korea, a little smaller than Washington state, hangs below North Korea which is bordered by China. Seoul, the capital of South Korea, is the center of political, economic, and cultural activity known for a gateway to the world. At the time of this writing, I've learned that for the past sixty years the adoption facilitators set up child welfare programs in this tiny nation and through this route sent 220,000 Korean children or more to new homes in mostly Western nations, such as the United States. Today, when it comes to adopting children from poorer nations, Africa is the new Asia.

I had expected South Korea to be more like the perspective given in *Seed from the East*, a memoir written by the adoption pioneer and evangelist Mrs. Holt: "In a country such as Korea, an amputee, unless helped by a missionary project, is doomed to the life of a beggar. To the Oriental, this is a life of shame and humiliation." She also wrote to her friends, "We saw before us the tragic plight of hundreds of illegitimate children . . .," and "Korea was a world of gutted buildings, shabby dwellings, starving children, lepers, and amputees," which jumped-started their adoption programs (otherwise known as "child protection measures" and child welfare for "the best interest of the child") worldwide.

Little would I know that Korea is also beautiful; full of sacred spots and consisting of moral and modest citizens. My perception on adoption flipped upside-down after listening the stories from other adoptees.

From Seoul to Incheon, Jenette and I travel by bus in the early evening over a skinny highway, past small rectangular cottages, swaying rice fields, and trees in the distance. Dark green hills roll into mountains with breathtaking peaks. We marvel at the scenery. The view of the rice paddies along the way soothe and calm our spirits while air conditioning gives relief from the sizzling and sultry August conditions.

For the last part of the tour, Korean adoptees take a short plane ride to *Jeju Do*, described on websites as the "Island of the Spirits" and "Home of the Gods," thanks to its bountiful landscape and native civilization. This is the largest island in South Korea, created entirely from volcanic eruptions about two million years ago. It consists of basalt, lava, and tropical foliage. Mt. Halla, located in the middle of the island, is the largest of 360 volcanoes, making it the highest point in the Republic of Korea. This is a premier destination, offering such stunning natural scenery as cliffs, waterfalls, and caves. Other amenities, such as golf courses, underwater exploration, horseback riding, wind surfing, fishing, and beach resorts make this a famous destination for honeymooners and overseas visitors.

THE "UNKNOWN" CULTURE CLUB

Large stone grandfathers (Tolharubang), carved from lava dot the island and tiny replicas are sold to tourists. In years past they were considered guardian deities and are currently available as elder husband and wife figurines. The two sets I buy are no larger than two inches in height and width. One couple is of a chubby man and woman in a kissing stance, lips puckered; the grandmother's eyes are closed and her elderly mate hides a bouquet of yellow flowers behind his back. The other couple eyes each other with suspiciously flirtatious smiles. To any normal onlooker, they might appear as a simple old, graying couple, but to me they represent the essence of ancient love, grandparents holding delightful secrets to local legends more than a thousand years old.

According to a museum there, the family structure was at one time matriarchal due to the "Sea Women," called *Haenyo*, often the head of the family. They dived to great depths without scuba gear, even holding their breath for more than two minutes to gather sea cucumbers, abalone, and conch, which were then sold to Japan for large profits. Because these women were the family's main breadwinners, men stayed home and raised the children. "In the 1950s there were up to 30,000 *Haenyo* 'sea divers' on the island. In 2003 there were only 5,650 women registered as divers, of whom 85 percent were over 50 years old." Local sea women can be seen around an unusual basalt rock formation, called "Dragon Rock" (*Yongduam*), molded by wind and waves.

Could our Korean mother be a "sea woman?" During the trip, I had hoped the newspaper articles written about our search would reach the island. Just in case they hadn't, Jenette and I still had the Korean namecards to pass out, which included our information and a message about our search.

Unable to sleep, I pull my hair into a long pony tail and leave the hotel room as the sun begins to rise. Jogging in the muggy warm breeze along the boardwalk makes my clothes sticky, but I enjoy the seaside aroma. Elderly Korean couples briskly walk along the cement and wood boardwalk. The light sun cascades across limitless blue water and the air is heavy and hot. *Jeju Do's* serene melody, combined with the quiet stirrings of couples, old and young, causes me to feel completely at home—as if I've always belonged here.

Korean Adoptees, Then and Now

A lighthouse sits on a rocky promontory about a mile away, luring me toward it like a magnetic force near the water's edge. It doesn't take long to reach a white tower near the sea. Reaching the point where jagged rocks meet walkway, I park myself on the edge to meditate, surrounded by the jade green mist and the endless sky. The sea glistens in the sunlight and the swish of waves lapping the shore mingles with the slapping of fishing lines hitting the water, thrown by old fishermen. Other Koreans practice Tai Ch'i next to the dock.

The ch'i moves thoughts through me. What would have happened if I had been brought up here? It's a question posed by many well-intentioned folks, implying that we would have ended up submissive and powerless if we had remained in South Korea.

But being over here has cast a magical spell. It's the first time I've ever felt total tranquility. It's the first time I can reflect on adoption clearly—without all the expectations placed on me by authorities who claim to know what's in the "best interest of the child."

There's a rumor about several suicides by members of our adoptee community: a Korean adoptee recently committed suicide during his first trip back to our homeland during the 2004 Korean Adoptee Gathering. Some assume it was due to being separated from his adoptive family—what the mainstream in the industry call our "real" family. Others suspect he wanted to leave his remains in the East Sea for all to see, making the point that an agency sold him off. I also heard about a twenty-three-year-old female adoptee who committed suicide after giving birth to her first child. And then, horribly, I was told about the 1984 suicide of Joseph Tae Holt, one of the adopted sons to married cousins and the pioneers of intercountry adoption, Harry and Bertha Holt. Devastatingly, no one was supposed to know about such news as it would stain the global and pioneering child welfare program. As the "adoptee" community, we were expected to keep positive about the practice of adoption and some of us were asked to go to the unwed mother homes and convince single mothers we had led successful lives in the West, leaving the impression that their babies would be well-cared for if only they would relinquish their rights of parenthood. I refused. The community, seen from a wider and deeper perspective began appearing like an assembly line to me—a cult in the making. I didn't want anything to do with it. Something inside prevented me from abiding by the system they had set up.

Some of us were asked to speak at agency fundraising events and write happy stories in their magazines to "keep things positive" even though we were kept away from policy-making boardroom chats and discussion roundtables. Within the last decade, I have noticed a few of us lucky ones are invited to the grand array as special guests to the (what some might call a toxic child-market) buffet. What started out as a 1953 charity has parboiled into a global production line, and I wonder if those who had committed suicide innately knew something was wrong with such the refined system, somewhere deep within their soul.

Rousing me from critical thoughts, an older gentleman near the water's edge climbs the large rocks with three giant steps to where I am sitting. Beside him, I gaze out to the water at a distant reflection. *Jeju Do*, known as a favorite retreat for honeymooners, casts a tender spell on its inhabitants. A few quiet moments pass before the man speaks to me although I cannot understand his words. I'm not sure how to respond, how to say "yes" or "no" in Korean, so I just smile and point to my heart. "I'm from America."

"Ah." He nods as if he knows. He probably assumes that because I got out of Korea, I'm one of the lucky ones. That's what I've always been told to believe.

Together, our gaze travels back out to the water and I wish that I could somehow communicate to him all I've been discovering. Do the Koreans know at all what it's like to grow up in the West with parents who cannot identify? It's certainly not Hollywood or Disneyland! But, at least, the discriminatory attitude against Asians has improved somewhat with time. I enjoy my life as an adult and have learned to adapt to the volatile environment. I appreciate the diversity finally blossoming in the United States. Opposing the practice of adoption would be considered disrespectful and we adoptees risk being persecuted for doing so—so for a good part of my life, I have ignored my own sorrows and abided. We're supposed to "be seen and not heard" on behalf of those who raise us.

The Korean man interrupts my thoughts. "Why?" He searches for English words finding only two, "Why? Why Korea?"

I try to explain, "*Omma*. To find *Omma*," is all I can say and wonder if *Omma* is the correct word for mother and whether or not I'm pronouncing it correctly. I reflect upon all I've learned during my time in Korea. The great majority of all Korean-born babies weren't even abandoned in the first place. To me, this changes everything. My mother could have been misinformed and misguided, in order to fill the West's demand for children. As a Korean mother of two daughters, it's hard to let go of the thought.

The curious gentleman grunts at my response, but neither of us understand each other. After a moment of simultaneous staring outward, he crawls over sharp rocks and heads for the boardwalk, leaving me to absorb the sights on this island that celebrates love. Previously, I would have assumed we had nothing in common. Today, I believe we have everything in common. My spirit is bolstered by the thought. My time in Seoul, the ancient history, the philosophies, the landscape, and its personality, rejuvenate me and I am one with nature.

The land of the morning calm hits me with radiance. I come to the realization that I must honor my SELF. By honoring my SELF, I honor my roots and the branches I have to hold onto. To me this means being receptive and identifying the situation with my own empathetic and informed eyes—and not the eyes of the adoptive mothers who did not approve of my search and wanted me to remain obedient and naive.

My time in Korea is coming to an end too quickly. Soon, I will be back in the States, assuming normal day-to-day responsibilities with Dad and my family. I have one more day on the island before we fly back, and I have a strange feeling. Maybe Omma recognized Jenette and me in the photo in the newspaper articles. Maybe she's seen us interviewed on television. If she's there, we'll only get one day—Korea's Freedom Day—to be with her. Maybe that's all we'll need to catch up. What does it feel like to have a Korean mother follow me around with a spoonful of kim chi and rice? Is it as bad as I've heard it is? Or would it be soothing and satisfying? What does it feel like to hear my Korean mother say "I want you" "I need you"?

    To adoption profiteers, this land is considered poverty stricken and the children must continue to be rescued even though the Korean War ended more than fifty years ago. The gates to intercountry adoption must remain open at all costs, even though agency workers haven't checked in with the exported children to see how they have faired—even fifty years later—or simply acknowledged the concerned voices of so many of us who have been scattered across the Western world. While agency workers continue to call the practice a miracle, I wonder now about my elderly Korean parents. Are they languishing on a Korean street corner? While I've been taking care of my adoptive father for the past thirty years, is anyone looking after my Korean parents? Or, because of my adoption overseas, are they now orphaned? I can't do nothing and call it peace.

✈ **JANINE MYUNG JA**
excerpt from
The Search For Mother Missing:
A Peek Inside International Adoption

AFTERTHOUGHTS

Thirty years ago, my twin and I had planned to open a Wellness Center inspired by our adoptive father. These plans, however, continue to be pushed further and further into the future due to pulling out more and more truths about exactly how children were obtained for adoption. We have found ourselves drowning in stories and experiences of pain, trauma and turmoil, witnessing as our soul sisters and brothers are called insulting names, told to behave and be thankful despite abuse, and watching as parents-of-loss are reduced to a function and stigmatized as "birthparents" in one lucrative swoop. As a consequence, industry builders have dismissed the pain, trauma, and grief of families—as if they do not exist at all. Community-based alternatives, which include tribal care, temporary and permanent guardianship, foster parenting, step-parenting, and other methods, that do not require an identity change or falsified documents, have been thrown out with the baby.

Agencies have had the first and final say on the "best interest of children" and "child protection." What have we learned from all of this? Continue to listen. By staying informed, we are less likely to be duped by the hidden agenda.

Korean Adoptees, Then and Now

Are we being positive? Not really. When we discuss systemic abuses, we do not need to sugarcoat unethical behaviors. A Pollyanna attitude disregards the suffering involved, and unresolved grief continues to grow and manifest until eventually, due to massive devastation, humanity is forced to pay attention. Let's enforce accountability, convince agencies to correct blatant past violations today—not tomorrow. Adult adopted people have a right to be given more information. *Now*. Discussions on filing a joint civil suit against a certain agency have been brought up several times by numerous adoptees.

Are we optimistic? *Yes*. We can be optimistic. Because of the information age, with more and more families reuniting, adult adopted people are becoming aware of their natural-born rights. As a result, younger generations can obtain more data, believe in their own capabilities, claim their rights, and better protect themselves against a veiled lucrative industry that thrives on naivety.

The stories included within this anthology are the mere tip of the iceberg, yet they are (sadly) typical. As more and more adopted people give themselves permission to speak, and as we follow the money, truth rises to the surface.

We have two choices: we can listen to the industry builders or we can listen to the families-of-loss. Policy-makers and adoption facilitators will claim children were unwanted or abandoned, and lead us to believe that adoptions are all good. They are afraid to admit that some were bad. If we do not recognize this, we'll stay in the shame that other people require us to feel in order for us to remain quiet ("seen but not heard") so they can justify their work.

When my twin and I first traveled back to Korea, we were stunned to learn not all adopted people live happily ever after. Typically, these voices have been verbally attacked and even persecuted. Questions, concerns, and opinions are too often ignored. After watching the community for more than a decade, we still believe these experiences need to be validated. We have come to the conclusion that those who resist the truth are those who cannot handle the truth.

✈ **THE VANCE TWINS**

ABOUT THE VANCE TWINS

The Vance twins have volunteered most of their free time to aid the Adoptee Rights Movement. In 2010, they cofounded Adoption Truth & Transparency Worldwide Network which now has almost 6000 interested members of mostly adult adopted people and parents or families of adoption-loss. These members have become empowered by connecting through social media. The online group, first intended to serve merely as a meeting place, news hub and family rights' advocacy space, has shed light on the hidden side of adoption and, ultimately, added *herstory* to adoption history.

Motivated by the public global dialogue and the shift in dynamic by adopted people, the twins were inspired to compile and produce *Adoptionland: From Orphans to Activists*. This anthology begins with personal accounts and then shifts to a bird's eye view on adoption from domestic, intercountry and transracial adoptees who are now adoptee rights activists. Along with adopted people, this collection also includes the voices of mothers and a father from the Baby Scoop Era, a modern-day mother who almost lost her child to adoption, and ends with the experience of an adoption investigator from Against Child Trafficking. These stories are usually abandoned by the very industry that professes to work for the "best interest of children," "child protection," and for families. However, according to adopted people who were scattered across nations as children, these represent typical human rights issues that have been ignored for too long. For many years, adopted people have just dealt with such matters alone, not knowing that all of us—as a community—have a great deal in common.

For the past sixty years, since the inception of adoption, many facilitators have avoided addressing unethical methods, leading to unnecessary separations and a stripping of true identity, immediate and extended family, potential community care, birth culture, family DNA and ancestry. Spreading awareness on the crisis of adoption trafficking comes with many rewards and it has potentially saved vulnerable at-risk local and global families from being exploited and falling victim to unethical adoption tactics, such as abduction, fraud, deception, abuse of power, and coercion.

The Vance Twins appreciate the investigational work and research of Against Child Trafficking (ACT), an international rights organization, promoting the correct interpretation and implementation of the United Nations Convention on the Rights of the Child (UNCRC). ACT legally represent families who have had crimes committed against them. Due to the little known crisis of trafficking and no agency accountability, ACT needs your help. In the effort to protect local and global families, stay informed, aware and share. Know your rights and tell your circle of friends and associates. ACT USA needs to educate local and global families, fund field research and investigate cases of exploited families, develop and distribute educational based materials, organize and participate in Child Rights based forums and related fields and provide professional and peer support for victims of trafficking.

It's never too late to walk in awareness
Stay connected and find the latest books and updates at
www.vancetwins.com
To stay informed on ACT's cases, go to
www.againstchildtrafficking.org
For news on industry practices, go to www.actusa.org

Against Child Trafficking is an international child rights organisation, registered in the Netherlands (Chamber of Commerce: 09183849). ACT's main focus is the prevention of child trafficking for intercountry adoption. ACT advocates child rights based social policies that are in compliance with the UN Convention on the Rights of the Child, which is the universal standard and the best safeguard against child trafficking.

ACT monitors intercountry adoption practices worldwide and conducts research on child rights issues, particularly those that effect children deprived of parental care and trafficked children.

ACT serves as Documentation & Research Center. The collected data serve local, regional and international child rights/human rights NGOs and networks, as well as individual child rights advocates and lawyers who deal with child trafficking issues, and of course the media.

ACT alerts international organisations and national governments to concrete cases of child trafficking for intercountry adoption.

ACT helps victims of child trafficking. We work together with local NGOs to find the trafficked children at the request of their parents, or to retrace the parents or extended family of trafficked adoptees.

These parents are mostly poverty stricken and living far away in the countryside. They may not have the means to travel to their country's main cities to file their cases, let alone to pay a lawyer. ACT also supports these parents and adoptees to take legal action.

ACT USA Recently formed ACT USA is a registered 501c 3 and supports the investigational and legal work of Against Child Trafficking.

- enable field research and investigate cases.
- Develop and spread educational materials based on the correct interpretation and proper implementation of the United Nations Convention on the Rights of the Child (UNCRC).
- Organize and participate in Child Rights based forums and related fields.
- Provide professional and peer support for victims of child trafficking

Excerpts from United Nations Conventions on Human Rights

on the Rights of the Child

Article 35 States Parties shall take all appropriate national, bilateral and multilateral measures to prevent the abduction of, the sale of or traffic in children for any purpose or in any form.

Article 36 States Parties shall protect the child against all other forms of exploitation prejudicial to any aspects of the child's welfare.

on the Prevention and Punishment of the Crime of Genocide

Adopted by Resolution 260 (III) A of the United Nations General Assembly on 9 December 1948.

Article 2, Paragraph 5: Forcibly transferring children of the group to another group

on the Indigenous Peoples

Adopted by the UN General Assembly during its 61st session at UN Headquarters in New York City on 13 September 2007

Article 31 Paragraph 1. "Indigenous peoples have the right to maintain, control, protect and develop their cultural heritage, traditional knowledge and traditional cultural expressions, as well as the manifestations of their sciences, technologies and cultures, including human and genetic resources, seeds, medicines, knowledge of the properties of fauna and flora, oral traditions, literatures, designs, sports and traditional games and visual and performing arts. They also have the right to maintain, control, protect and develop their intellectual property over such cultural heritage, traditional knowledge, and traditional cultural expressions." CITEREFUN200811

on Drugs and Crime

Article 3, Paragraph (a) of the Protocal to Prevent, Suppress and Punish Trafficking in Persons defines Trafficking in Persons as the recruitment, transportation, transfer, harbouring or receipt of persons, by means of the threat or use of force or other forms of coercion, of abduction, of fraud, of deception, of the abuse of power or of a position of vulnerability or of the giving or receiving of payments or benefits to achieve the consent of a person having control over another person, for the purpose of exploitation. Exploitation shall include, the exploitation of the prostitution of others or other forms of sexual exploitation, forced labour or services, slavery or practices similar to slavery, servitude or the removal of organs and other forms of exploitation.

CARING AND SHARING PREVENTS ADOPTION TRAFFICKING

WHO WE ARE

Adoption Truth & Transparency Worldwide Network Social Media Group consists of concerned citizens who care about and want to protect children. Everyone is invited to join. We are a diverse group of researchers, authors, stay-at-home parents, students, professionals and retirees. We come from all over the world, unified by our optimism to educate the public on the dangers of intercountry adoption for the purpose child trafficking or sexual exploitation. Many of us have been adopted, or belong to a family of adoption-loss. Some of us are adoptive parents. All of us agree that various forms of child trafficking hurt families and children. The purpose of this group has been to primarily educate the public on the problem of adoption trafficking.

HOW WE PROTECT FAMILIES

The first steps to protecting families is receptivity, empathy, understanding, and awareness. By forming a coalition of caring individuals from diverse backgrounds and with the network of other adoption and anti-trafficking organizations, we can prevent adoption trafficking. Spreading awareness about all forms of trafficking is key to our success. Together, we are empowered to provide real child protection for local and global communities.

We appreciate the help of volunteers who care about adoption trafficking victims. We have listened and learned as much as possible, shared news articles on the issue, and have spoken about unaddressed and unresolved adoption cases. We are motivated by the investigational and research work of Against Child Trafficking based in Brussels, Belgium and registered in the Netherlands.

WHEN DOES CHILD TRAFFICKING OCCUR

Usually child trafficking occurs in rural areas all over the world—including the United States. Young single-parent families who are considered illiterate or poverty-stricken are the prime targets for adoption trafficking. Child traffickers ignore correct interpretation and implementation of the United Nations Convention on the Rights of the Child (UNCRC) and other binding agreements which protect women and children, such as the United Nations Protocol to Prevent, Suppress and Punish Trafficking in Persons.

Also Available from the Vance Twins
www.vancetwins.com

Books by Janine Myung Ja
The rEvolutionary Orphan Series

Based on the Vance Twins' Life
*Twins Found in a Box:
Adapting to Adoption*

*The Search for Mother Missing:
A Peek Inside International Adoption*

Anthologies
*Adoptionland:
From Orphans to Activists*

*The "Unknown" Culture Club:
Korean Adoptees, Then and Now*

Empowerment
*Master Adoption:
From an Angry Ajumma*

Feature Length Screenplays

For the Love of Children:
In 1969, an all-American couple adopts an infant from overseas and raises the girl with good old-fashioned family values. Years later they learn she might not be the orphan they imagined her to be.

Rebirth:
A young transracially adopted teenager's untimely pregnancy in the late 1980's sends shockwaves throughout the church community and especially devastates her loving adoptive mother. The young adoptee must choose between doing the right thing or abiding by her own quiet guidance.

Forever Family:
A middle-age adult adoptee is shocked when she learns that she is not a U.S. citizen—and never was. To make matters worse, her birth family wants to reunite with her. Despite being tempted to travel overseas and learn the truth about her birth, she is forced to remain in the states and stay loyal to her loving adoptive parents.

All for Mom:
An eager-to-please adult adoptee learns her loving elderly Caucasian adoptive mother—a hoarder and a widow—is being kicked out of her home due to 'squalor' conditions. The adoptee opens an adult family home business in a gigantic effort to make her mother happy. But the business makes the adoptee miserable.

Colorblind:
When an intercountry adoptee contemplates marriage with a man of the same race, her proud colorblind adoptive mother makes certain to voice her opinion, intent on saving the adoptee's life.

Adoption Bonds:
When an adult adoptee (and previous proud advocate of international adoption) learns that her daughter has a mysterious disease affecting her health, she digs into her past to help, but gets stonewalled by the adoption agency. She must decide which side she wants to believe in and how to handle the truth.

Identity Crisis:
Both adoptive mother and adoptee daughter must learn how to adapt to life's ever-changing roles of caregiver and caretaker. Added to this challenge, middle-age daughter must re-invent herself in an effort to fulfill a wish to speak on behalf of her mother.

*Screenplays can be adapted to be made in the United States or in global markets and tailored to the nationality of the producer and director's preferences. Ten percent of any profit is given to the individual who personally connects Janine with the producer. These scripts have been registered with the US Copyright Office and with Writer's Guild of America (WGA), West.

Are you looking for an expert on adoption, Metaphysics, or the Asian-American experience? Need help developing and adding depth to your minority characters? Contact Janine at: **info@vancetwins.com**.

THE ORPHAN'S MOUNT
✈ *Janine Myung Ja*

✈
Lucky.
Be quiet.
Little thief.
Say, thank you.
Quit watching me.
What do you know?
Don't bother me now.
Go back to your room.
You should be grateful.
Who do you think you are?
You're making me nervous.
You are not a *real* American.
All children deserve families.
Do not speak until spoken to.
We know what is best for you.
Nothing beats the United States.
You should be ashamed of yourself.
This hurts me more than it hurts you.
Chinks, go back to where you came from.
So many orphans are *waiting* to be adopted.
Koreans have a fascination with blood ties.
All you have to do is accept the blood of Jesus
What are you? No, like, what nationality are you?
That's an immature way of looking at the situation.
After all we've done for you, how dare you disobey.
You would have been a whore if you stayed in Korea.
You need permission from your adoptive parents to search

---

for your
Korean
Family.

"Let's be Friends!"
For updates or to interview the contributors,
friend the twins on the *Vance Twins* Facebook Page.

Made in the USA
San Bernardino, CA
16 July 2015